ON THE FIFTH DAY

A.J. WATSON

Adogsviewtraining.com
357Press.com

Copyright Anna Watson 2018
Library of Congress Congressional Number Pending as of publication. Visit 357 Press for updates.

Published by 357 Press, Atlanta Georgia

ISBN 13: 978-0-9896172-5-3

Non-fiction
Religion
Historical
Animal Welfare

Edited by Mary-Elizabeth Watson

Cover Design by W.M. DeSilva

Authors Note - 9

Introduction - 11

Part I

-In the beginning -16

-After the fall - 44

-The covenant - 70

-Noachide and Mosaic laws - 85

-Imitatio Dei - 107

Part II

-Historical treatment of animals - 122

-The Middle Ages and Animal Sentience - 143

-The Industrial Revolution - 159

-Modern trends - 175

-Psychology behind the bond -197

Epilogue -222

Glossary - 229

Author's note

You will notice throughout the course of this book the frequent use of the word "myth." Many people have a negative connotation with the word and automatically think of Santa Claus or the Easter Bunny. However, myth in this context is used in the academic sense describing a sacred story; passed down in tradition, and used to describe the early history of a people and their world views. Some people cling to the negative connotations surrounding the word and take offense when beliefs they hold true are described as myths. However, the author makes no claim as to the fact or fiction of any myth mentioned, and leaves it up to the reader to believe as they wish.

Scientific ideals and theories are presented periodically during the course of this book. It is the author's belief that science and religion complement each other. The Christian and Hebrew Bible tells us quite often that God intended for his presence to be known. God gave man fully developed frontal lobes, a curiosity about the natural world, and a drive to learn. Through scientific inquiry and investigation we can learn exactly how God created the universe, how each section of our brains work, and other such phenomena. Through the study of religion we can learn why God created the universe, why we have such fully developed brains in relation to other animals, and other such phenomena. It is therefore necessary to present both scientific research and religious theology in order to make the case for the uniqueness of animals and their place in the universe.

Throughout this book you will notice the word "animal" rather than the more current phrase "nonhuman animal." Obviously humans are classified as animals as well; however, only rarely is the phrase "nonhuman animal" used in this book. This is due to the author's recognition of the inherent value of animals in their own right. Rather than describe them as what they are not, it is best to just leave them as they are: special, unique, and loved by God.

All Biblical verses were taken from the New International Version of the Holy Bible.

INTRODUCTION

When I was 8 months old, my parents were given a Standard Poodle puppy named Ebony's Brown Trick, which they later shortened to "Trixie." From there I was hooked. From an early age I insisted on being the one to care for her, feed her, and walk her. I felt that if I did all of that then she would be "mine." It didn't occur to me that I could still play with her and love her without all the extra responsibility. In my childish mind I didn't want to share her with my brother and sisters. She died when I was 14. I was 28 before I could even look at another Standard Poodle.

As a teenager I noticed that dogs transcend cultures. There isn't much that crosses cultural divides, yet dogs manage this feat. I took note of that as evidence that dogs must be something special. I didn't trust people that didn't like dogs. Even Hitler had a German Shepherd named Blondi, and Genghis Khan had hundreds of mastiffs; if those guys, men who were widely regarded as evil, loved dogs, what kind of people *didn't* like them? Years later I learned that a love of dogs is actually in our DNA. When the earliest men first went stumbling around on this planet, some early wolves started hanging around them. Wolves who were too aggressive were killed and those who were too shy lost the hunting advantage and protection provided by man. They died and their genes did not get passed on. Early man who did not like dogs lost the hunting advantage and protection provided by wolves. Likewise, they also died and their genes did not get passed on.

Cross-species kinship was bred into us, dogs more than any other species, bond closer to humans than to their own kind.

Over time, these select wolves lost strength in their jaws, their brains decreased in size, their diets changed, and they became diurnal. While this was happening, man began to change as well. Our sense of smell decreased, our brains have gotten smaller[1], and we can no longer wiggle our ears. Both species evolved to depend on each other. Our love of dogs became human nature. A beautiful relationships has evolved between dog and man, and I see the hand of God behind it.

Dogs are special because dogs and humans evolved together, but they aren't the only animal we feel kinship with. It wasn't long before we turned our attention to the domestication of other animals; namely, cats and livestock. We've altered their evolution, and they've altered ours. At any given moment, a cat video is being played online. Culturally, cats have been adored in Japan, the Middle East, Egypt, India, and North America. This adoration dates back thousands of years.

Cars have rendered the horse and buggy obsolete, yet still today millions of horses are kept as pets, used for tours, and even assist police work. Rats and ferrets have been used to lay guide wires. Rats have also been used to detect land mines, saving countless lives in the process. Animals as diverse as pigs and miniature horses to reptiles have been used as therapy animals and have been proven to lower our blood pressure.

---

[1] There are many theories why are brains have shrunk since the Stone Age; but a prevailing theory is that the smaller size is proof that we've "tamed" ourselves. Similar trends are also found in other domestic animals; sheep, pigs, cattle, and dogs.

We reap the benefits of animals every day. Unfortunately, they sometimes suffer due to our interactions. Every year nearly 60 billion animals are killed for human consumption. This number does not include animals who are hunted or fished for sport. There are no exact figures on animals for commercial fishing. Estimates range from 970-2700 billion wild caught and from 37-129 billion farmed fish that are killed annually. (2)

Between 100,000-200,000 rabbits, guinea pigs, mice, rats, and hamsters are killed (3) for cosmetics testing. Pharmacological testing kills more than 115 million dogs, cats, miniature pigs, and guinea pigs. The United States does not include birds; fish, rats, mice, amphibians, reptiles, and invertebrates in their official counts. However, these animals make up 90% of all tested species. Therefore, the official count of 115 million is substantially lower than reality.

It's easy to ignore the previous paragraphs; it's nothing more than a series of numbers. In fact, nearly 7 billion people on the planet ignore it every day. The truth is, it's much easier to ignore it than it is to confront it. We convince ourselves that the aforementioned deaths are numbers, not lives. There is a well-known phenomenon in psychology (4) coined the "collapse of compassion." Essentially, it means that when the number of victims in a tragedy increases, our sympathy decreases, or even disappears altogether. This appears to be a defense mechanism in humans. One death is tragic, two deaths should be twice as tragic, 115 million deaths should be 115 million times more tragic. Our hearts can't handle that, so they simply tune it out. In our minds, the tragedy disappears. Unfortunately, so does our motivation to do anything to help.

Mother Teresa once said "If I look at the mass, I will never act." On that note, I introduce you to CH-377.

CH-377, a chimpanzee who was renamed "Pablo" by the Fauna Foundation who rescued him, died at the age of 30, half the lifespan of a captive chimp. During his time at the Fauna Foundation, he displayed a number of behavioral and emotional problems due to the previous torment he had suffered during his short life. Had he lived a normal lifespan, he may have overcome his issues. Sadly, he died before he got that chance. Born in 1970, he traveled the carnival circuit with two other chimps until they were all three given to the Institute for Primate Studies in 1981, when Pablo was 11.[5] His teeth were removed or cut down to the gum line, not uncommon in the entertainment industry. This was a physical act of cruelty, the first of many physical and visible scars he was to receive at the hands of man.

From 1981 until 1997, Pablo was used by the New York University Laboratory for Experimental Medicine and Surgery in Primates. Housed in a 5x5x7 foot cage, the 300 pound chimp was only ever allowed to leave the enclosure for experiments. Joseph D'Agnese of *Discover Magazine* wrote that Pablo "had been darted 220 times....He had been subjected to 28 liver, two bone marrow, and two lymph node biopsies. His body was injected four times with vaccines, one of them known to be hepatitis vaccine; in 1993 he was injected with 10,000 times the lethal dose of HIV."[6] However, it wasn't the HIV that killed him; he died of an infection brought on by years of mistreatment, biopsies, and injections. [7]

As Pablo began to deteriorate, the sanctuary's owners, Gloria Grow and Richard Allan, fought desperately to save

Pablo, but it wasn't enough. On October 6, 2001, he succumbed to his illness and died. A tearful Grow allowed the other chimps at the sanctuary to view Pablo's body. His fellow chimpanzees groomed him, rubbed his belly, opened his eyes, and tried to wake him. When they realized that he would never wake again; they wandered off howling, hooting, screaming, and pounding their steel surroundings, mourning the loss of their friend. Pablo lived a tragic life in isolation, and for sixteen years he suffered, subjected to tremendous abuse. But his last few years he was loved.

He didn't die alone in a steel cage, the fate of so many before him. He died at a sanctuary, beloved by chimps and humans alike. His steel enclosure, too small to move around in, was replaced by an enriched environment that mimicked his natural habitat. The torturous experiments had been replaced by medical treatments, designed to save his life and ease his pain, where before he had been isolated, he finally had been given companionship, freedom, and love. His last few years, Pablo had finally found relief from the fear, pain, and the hardship he had previously known. In the end, he had finally found a home.

Gloria Grow wrote of his death that "Providing a loving and safe home for Pablo, if even for a short time, is one of my greatest accomplishments." Both humans and chimpanzees mourned his death. Most research chimps weren't that lucky; over 90% lived and died in the labs. Some of Pablo's ashes were scattered around the sanctuary. The rest were taken by Jane Goodall to Gombe forest in Tanzania, where he now rests, forever free from the punishing hand of man.

Pablo's story is tragic, but there is a happy ending. For more than 25 years, wild chimpanzees have been listed as "endangered" under the Endangered Species Act. Yet, due to a loophole, captive chimps were considered merely "threatened" and research was allowed to continue on our closest cousins. In 2015, the U.S. Fish and Wildlife Service (FWS) changed the status of captive chimps, designating them endangered. This means that chimpanzees can no longer be used for research.

The U.S. National Institute of Health (NIH) had already begun the process of phasing them out of laboratories in 2013. NIH director Francis Collins stated "... new scientific methods and technologies have rendered [the chimps'] use in research largely unnecessary." With new technologies for testing medications becoming increasingly available and growing opposition from activists, all animal testing will hopefully one day be obsolete. This new law by the FWS closes any remaining legal loopholes and will keep chimps safe in the future, while the Humane Society may redirect their focus to save the remaining test animals.

The hand of God is behind the more positive aspects of our relationship with animals. Our inhumane treatment of animals and our lack of concern for their well-being is an indictment on humanity. But the story doesn't end there. We are guilty of terrible atrocities, and at the same time, we commit incredible acts of kindness. Pablo spent his entire life suffering, enduring cruel torture and abuse from people, while humanity turned a blind eye to his pain. Yet at the end, he was ultimately saved by the same species who harmed him; those Good Samaritans who dedicated their lives to extending mercy to the least of their brothers and sisters.

We are related to animals; to some more closely than to others. We're built from the same parts. From the dust we all came, so to the dust we will all return. Billions of species breathing the same air and drinking the same water, all sharing the same planet. As a species we're not alone after all. On a gut level we all feel the same call of the wild. How empty Earth would be if humans were the sole inhabitants. God saw fit to fill the Earth with wondrous variety. Despite our differences, we're all connected on a spiritual level, and it is a beautiful thing.

PART I

Religion and Animal Welfare

CHAPTER I

IN THE BEGINNING

And God made the beasts of the Earth according to their kinds, and the livestock according to their kinds, and everything that creeps on the ground according to its kind. And God saw that it was good.
Genesis 1:25

Picture it: eons ago, darkness. Then God said "Let there be light." Nothing, then something. Before the Earth was fully created, God saw fit to fill it with all kinds of living things. He made it self-sustaining: the plants convert sunlight into oxygen; through photosynthesis atmospheric oxygen is maintained and enough energy is supplied for life on Earth. After the creation of flora, God created the 'living creatures according to their kind,' and then he created male and female. God blessed them and instructed them to rule over the fish in the sea and the birds in the sky and over all the mammals, reptiles, and amphibians on land. Genesis 1:29-30 tells us that God said *"I give you every seed-bearing plant on the face of the Earth and every tree that has fruit with seed in it. They will be yours for food. And to all the beasts of the Earth and all the birds in the sky and all the creatures that move along the ground- everything that has the breath of life in it- I give every green plant for food."*

This is curious. Most of the Biblical account of creation aligns almost perfectly with the current scientific theory of the Big Bang. Sometime between nine and fifteen billion years ago

God spoke and the universe began. Out of nothing, there was something. Then the sun and the Earth were formed about 4.5 billion years ago, when God said "Let there be light." After that was the creation and separation of water, science tells us that protoplanets and asteroids collided with the Earth to bring this water. This happened approximately 4.4 billion years ago, on the Biblical second day.

Over the next several billion years the Earth cooled, water condensed, clouds were formed, and water on Earth was separated from water in the atmosphere. 2.7 billion years ago oxygen was first produced, and 2.45 billion years ago, it began to stabilize in our atmosphere. At around the same time, oxygen reacted with seawater, leaving behind evidence in the form of oxidized iron in the sea floor we see here that God is patient and takes His time. From there came the creation of sea life, formed 635 million years ago (single celled bacteria came a couple billion years before that.)

Land eventually separated from water. According to science, the oceans and land began to separate about 3.75 billion years ago, on the third day of creation. And finally God created birds, all the other animals, and man. Life began in the sea and made its way on to land. On the fifth day, God created sea life and on the sixth day God created all other life. This is in line with science; life began in the waters and eventually moved on to land, with mankind being the last link in the chain of life. So far, so good. Is it a coincidence that the early authors of the Bible knew that? Or did some Divine source inform them?

The creation story in the Bible, with a few exceptions, is in line with our current understanding of science. Depending, of course, on how literally one takes the meaning of the word "day." According to 2 Peter, with God "A day is like a thousand years, and a thousand years is like a day." Notice he uses the simile "like." God is beyond time, He has no need for mere human clocks and calendars. What really differs in the creation account from our understanding of the Big Bang, is the early vegan diet.

Leaving aside that Genesis tells us that all life was vegan, how well does a vegan diet square with our current beliefs about early man? On the surface it would be easy to dismiss this as fiction. Dietary fads, such as Atkins and the Paleo diet, are based on the belief that the human body was designed to eat meat and that our ancestors were fine-tuned hunting machines. There is widespread belief that eating meat gave our ancestors the extra energy needed to help develop our complex brains and push us ahead of other great apes. In other words, our carnivorous diet made us human.

However, our brains, as complex and powerful as they are, are not the only body part; there are many parts that make a body whole. We also need a long digestive tract, healthy livers and kidneys, and a whole slew of other body parts to function, thrive, and reproduce. New research [1] shows that carbohydrates played a key part in the development of early man. Karen Hardy, of the Catalan Institute for Research and Advanced Studies, believes that cooked starch provided the increase in energy needed for organs and tissue with high glucose demands; the brain, red blood cells, and developing fetuses. Once built, our brain does not require extra protein.

Dr. Richard Leakey, paleoanthropologist and one of Africa's leading conservationists, also believes that early man ate a primarily vegetarian diet. Leakey stated that "You can't tear flesh by hand, you can't tear hide by hand, and we wouldn't have been able to deal with the food sources that require those large canines." Leakey believed that our earliest ancestors were scavengers when they could find meat, but that earliest man thrived on a primarily plant-based diet. (2) This is in line with current archeological evidence. Archeology seems to align with the Biblical account of veganism.

Paleontologists who study fossil remains and anthropologists who study indigenous people believe that meat only made up about 30% of the hunter-gatherer's diet. Sometimes they ate more, other times they ate less. Excluding the Inuit, who eat meat about 99% of the time, the success rate of modern indigenous hunters is less than 50%. Given that early man didn't have the same equipment as modern tribes; it is easy to believe that their success rate was even lower.

It would have been much easier for a caveman to grab a handful of berries than for him to kill a rhinoceros with sticks and stones. Further evidence shows that starch granules from plants have been found on fossilized teeth and tools. Humans may have been eating grains and tubers for the past 100,000 years or so. As you can see, there is much evidence for a primarily vegetarian diet in early man. Once again, Genesis is in line with science.

Some paleoanthropologists have looked at the stomachs, rather than the stomach contents, to find evidence of what our earliest ancestors ate. Our stomachs are quite unremarkable and differ little from the stomachs of our primate cousins. A simple stomach (if something as complex and efficient as a stomach can be called simple) breaks down protein, absorbs sugars, and ferments leftover plant material. The digestive tract of a carnivore is short, but their stomachs are rather large. Their stomachs contain an enzyme with hydrochloric acid ten times more powerful than that of an herbivore.

By comparison, the digestive tract of herbivores is long and their stomachs are small. While a carnivore's stomach contains more enzymes, in herbivores and humans it's the saliva that contains more digestive enzymes. Other primates, with stomachs quite like ours, eat mainly fruits, leaves, and nuts, supplemented by the occasional grubs and insects. Our earliest ancestors may not have been vegetarian by choice, but we cannot ignore the evidence that they consumed more plant than animal based foods. For those keeping count: Bible two, Science two. They're not actually in competition.

Now, before we get too caught up on vegetarianism versus omnivorism, the biggest thing that we need to remember is that early man didn't just eat one food. One of the reasons for the success of our species may be our ability to thrive on any diet. Our omnivorism means that we can survive on a variety of foods. It does not necessarily mean that those foods will be beneficial to us in the long run, but in the short term it will meet our needs and keep us alive long enough to pass on our genes. This is a rather beneficial trait in the fight for survival of the fittest, and the entire point of evolution in a nutshell.

****

The biggest question though is not *did early man eat meat?* Rather the important thing to ask is *why did the Bible instruct vegetarianism?* To be sure, other religions follow vegetarian diets. Hindus are known for keeping a traditionally vegetarian diet. They are often stereotyped as total vegetarians, and they have a great variety of vegetarian dishes. However, stereotypes do not necessarily reflect the reality. 71.6% of the male and 70.7% of the female population of India (4) regularly consume meat. This is no recent fad; when the religion was first founded, sometime around 2000 BCE, its members saw no reason to abstain from flesh. Their idea of an afterlife was based on a merit system and those who sacrificed animals were more likely to gain favor. (5) In the sixth century BCE, Buddhism and Jainism emerged and the value they placed on life had a profound influence on Hinduism.

Buddhism and Jainism were both born in India from the Hindu religion. Buddhists base their beliefs on the teachings of Siddārtha Guatama, the first Buddha. While Jains base their beliefs on the teachings of Mahavira, the most recent *Tirthankara* (a wise teacher sent to lead the world to moksha; freedom from samsara, the cycle of death and rebirth.) Both Mahavira and Buddha Guatama were born as princes. Mahavira was born into the Warrior Caste as Vardhamāna in 599 BCE, although that date is subject to debate.

When he was thirty his parents King Siddhartha and Queen Trishla passed away. After their deaths Vardhamāna renounced the throne and lived as an ascetic. Some traditions claim he married a woman named Yashoda and had an infant daughter; other traditions state he went against his parents' wishes and never married. In either case, Yashoda did not accompany him on his journey to spiritual perfection. For over a decade he fasted and meditated, eventually achieving enlightenment. From then on he was known as Mahavira, which means Great Victor.

Likewise, Siddārtha Gautama was born into the warrior caste in 566 BCE, though scholars debate the accuracy of this date. He was born to King Suddhodana and Queen Maya.

Shortly after he was born, Maya died and Siddhārtha was raised by his aunt Mahapajapati Gotami. As a child, Siddhārtha was sheltered from all pain and suffering. He ventured into the real world at the age of twenty-nine and for the first time witnessed a sick man, an old man, and a dead man. This had a profound effect on the prince who realized that his wealth and privilege could not save him from illness, age, and death.

This new knowledge disturbed Prince Siddhārtha so much that he renounced his throne, left his wife and infant son, and lived as an ascetic for more than half a decade. During this period, he gained followers, deprived himself of all worldly possessions, fasted to the point of near starvation, and even refused to drink water. After such extreme fasting, he was offered a bowl of rice, and upon taking it, he realized that such deprivations were not necessary. His followers, believing that he had abandoned his aestheticism, left him. However, he had not abandoned his beliefs, they had merely evolved. This led to his belief in the Middle Way, which sought balance between opulence and suffering. Siddhārtha sat beneath a sacred fig tree (this later became the *Bodhi Tree,* or tree of awakening) and meditated until dawn. It was there that he achieved enlightenment and became a Buddha, one who has attained perfect enlightenment.

Both Buddhism and Jainism emerged during a time of religious turmoil within the Hindu religion. New schools of philosophy and religion were challenging traditional beliefs. The Vedas (ancient Hindu scriptures) were being met with skepticism and derision, and many began to outright reject the Vedic traditions. Culturally, it was the perfect setting for a new religious movement. The Buddha and Mahavira were both charismatic men who attracted a large following of tens of thousands of followers. Both sages taught non-violence to living things. This idea caught on with contemporary Hindu leaders who began to emphasize a more ethical lifestyle and diet. This pushed the idea of vegetarianism back into mainstream Hindu consciousness.

Throughout the history of Hinduism, vegetarianism waxed and waned, often connected to beliefs of reincarnation and even at times tied to complexities within the caste system. Some scriptures encourage moderate diets, but the motivation seems to be to encourage the faithful to exercise restraint and self-control, not necessarily concern for animal welfare. The Hindu sages believe that vegetarianism can help maintain a balance between mind and body. While some scriptures show more compassion for the animals, the Vedas on the other hand, show how the gods Indra and Agni had a preference for bulls and cows as sacrifice.

Rig Veda CXI.2 *For sacrifice make for us active, vital power for skill, wisdom, and food with noble progeny. Grant to our company this most excellent power, that we may dwell with a heroic family.* And in book ten, hymn CXI.14-15 states that *He in whom horses, bulls, oxen, and barren cows, and rams, when duly set apart are offered up,- To Agni, Soma-sprinkled, drinker of sweet juice, Disposer, with my heart I bring a fair hymn forth. Into thy mouth is poured the offering, Agni, as Soma into cup, oil into ladle. Vouchsafe us with wealth. Strength-winning, blest with heroes, wealth lofty, praised by men, and full of splendor.* Later Brahminical texts tell us how the cow is food. Rig Veda Book ten, LXXXVI. 14 *Fifteen in number, then, for me a score of bullocks they prepare, and I devour the fat thereof: they fill my belly full with food. Supreme is Indra over all.*

It seems that while a vegetarian diet is encouraged, meat-eating is permitted, and indeed, the norm, and sacrifice will please the gods. Regardless of all that, Hinduism does have a deserved reputation as a religion that promotes a vegetarian diet, even while most of its adherents eat meat. Mohandas Gandhi once famously said "To my mind, the life of a lamb is no less precious than that of a human being. I should be unwilling to take the life of a lamb for the sake of a human body." Statements like this are why Hindus are stereotyped as vegetarian. Both vegetarian Hindus and those who follow a more meat-based diet cite scripture in support of their preference. The Rig-Veda, Book ten, hymn LXXXVII (16-19) states rather harshly that:

The fiend who smears himself with the flesh of cattle, with flesh of horses and of human bodies, who steals the milk cows milk away, O Agni- tear off the heads of such with fiery fury. The cow gives milk each year, O Man-regarder, let not the Yātudhāna ever taste it. If one would glut him with the biesting, Agni, pierce with thy flame his vitals as he meets thee. Let the fiends drink the poison of the cattle; may Aditi cast off the evildoers. May the God Savitar give them up to ruin, and be their share of plants and herbs denied them. Agni, from days of old thou slates the demons: never shall Rāksasas in fight overcome thee. Burn up the foolish ones, the flesh-devourers: let none of them escape thine heavenly arrow.

And Manu Samhita (the code of laws of Manu, the first man) 5:45-48: *He who injures harmless beings from a wish to (give) himself pleasure, never finds happiness, neither* living nor dead. He who does not seek to cause the sufferings of bonds and death to living creatures, (but) desires the good of all (beings), obtains endless bliss. He who does not injure any (creature), attains without effort what he thinks of, what he undertakes, and what he fixes his mind on. Meat can never be obtained without injury to living creatures, and injury to sentient beings is detrimental to (the attainment of) heavenly bliss; let him therefore shun the use of meat.*

The afore mentioned sutras[2], and other similar sutras, deliver a powerful statement against a meat-based diet. They also simultaneously show how militant some people can be about their diets. The above passages are often used to justify vegetarianism and compassionate living for Hindus. While the slaughter of animals for sacrifice was encouraged, the slaughter of animals for one's own pleasure is a sin.

Hindu vegetarians who follow these scriptures believe that though a vegetarian diet is desired, meat-eating is a concession to those who feel they cannot stop eating meat. A concession that God himself makes later in the Biblical book of Genesis. Hinduism is not a dogmatic religion. They believe that everybody has a different capacity to follow their own spiritual path. Even if that path leads them to devour animal flesh. The purpose behind abstaining from meat appears to be not for the welfare of the animals, but for greater spiritual awareness and practice for Hindus. A marked difference from the Genesis command for vegetarianism.

****

---

[2] rules summarizing the Vedic doctrines

Buddhism, though it had great influence on the vegetarian and vegan trends in Hinduism, was another religion that permitted the consumption of meat. It is said that Gautama Buddha died after eating pork, though there is considerable debate surrounding the legend. We do know that the Buddha died after eating a dish called 'suukaramaddava;' what is unclear, however, is the translation of that word. Some believe it was a mushroom, while others claim it was pork.

Whether it was meat or not is of little importance. As Siddhārtha Gautama was not a vegetarian after his enlightenment; he broke no rules by eating either dish. Buddhism teaches freedom from desire; it was therefore a common practice for early Buddhist monks to wander from village to village with a begging bowl. They ate what was given to them without choice or complaint, whether it was meat, or vegetables and grains.

As Buddhism evolved they developed a code for monks which included dietary regulation. Humans, elephants, and horses were deemed too noble to eat. Dogs, snakes, lions, tigers, leopards, bears, and hyenas were seen as too repulsive or dangerous.[6] All raw meat was forbidden, and monks weren't permitted to eat meat that was specifically killed for them. Although tradition allows Buddhists to eat meat, a minority, particularly the Mahayana Buddhists, still choose to abstain. Geography plays a large role in the diet of both monks and lay people. Vegetarianism is more common among Chinese and Vietnamese Buddhists, than among those residing in Tibet or Japan.

Meanwhile, Jains could be the poster religion for ethical dietary laws. They follow strict *Ahimsa* (non-violence to all living things). Jainism had a profound influence on vegetarianism in Buddhist and Hindu lifestyles. Since its inception 2,600 years ago, Jains have maintained their commitment to compassionate living. Jains take great care not to hurt insects, or even microorganisms in their daily lives. The faithful will sweep the walkways in front of them to avoid crushing any life forms while they walk. In addition to abstaining from meat, Jains will not eat vegetables that have to be uprooted, or textured vegetables that may trap insects. While many modern Jains may not be as strict on their diet as the more orthodox ones, most Jains still follow a strict vegan diet.

****

Other religions, from Zoroastrianism, to Taoism, to the Baha'i, have also encouraged compassion for animals and a more vegetable based diet. Therefore, it's not unusual that the God of Abraham would command the same. As with the Eastern traditions, vegetarianism may have been the ideal, but it is not widely practiced among the everyday adherents of the faith. Those with a keen eye will note the language of the Biblical text. After God created the greenery of the Earth, he proclaimed it "good." After he created the animals, he said that it was "good." And God created male and female in his image and he blessed them to be fruitful and multiply. He gave them dominion over the animals.

Then God said, "I give you every seed-bearing plant on the face of the whole Earth and every tree that has fruit with seed in it. They will be yours for food. And to all the beasts of the Earth and all the birds of the air and all the creatures that move on the ground – everything that has breath of life in it- I give every green plant for food." And it was so. God saw all that he had made and it was **very** good. [Genesis 1:29-31 NIV]

God was pleased with his creation, saying that it was good. Yet the peaceful harmony in which we lived in Eden was very good. The original Judaeo/Christian/Islamic ideal was harmony and community with all life. In Genesis 2:18 God said that it was not good that man should be alone, so he brought all the animals to Adam for him to name. Animals were the very first companion of humanity. Only then did God create Eve to be Adam's helpmate. After the fall of man and the flood, meat was permitted with limitations. However, despite that concession, every Biblical Utopia includes a vegan world. When describing the new heavens and new Earth, Isaiah 65:25 states that:

"The wolf and the lamb will feed together, and the lion will eat straw like the ox, but dust will be the serpents's food. They will neither hunt nor destroy on all my holy mountain." Says the LORD.

And in chapter 11:6-9, prophesying about the Messianic age, Isaiah writes:

The wolf will live with the lamb and the leopard will lie down with the goat, the calf and the lion and the yearling together; and a little child will lead them. The cow will feed with the bear, their young will lie down together, and the lion will eat straw like the ox. The infant will play near the hole of the cobra, and the young child put his hand into the viper's nest. They will neither harm nor destroy on my holy mountain, for the Earth will be full of the knowledge of the LORD as the waters cover the sea.

God's original plan for us, and His ultimate ideal, as described in Isaiah and elsewhere, is a world without bloodshed. Of course, we all know how that ended. Humans had only been on Earth for two generations when the first murder was committed, thereby setting the stage for more violence and depravity to come. After the flood, God gave mankind permission to consume flesh. Mankind had fallen by then and proved himself unworthy of the high ideals God had originally intended in Eden.

While God conceded permission to eat meat, it was not a buffet of any and all animals without restrictions. Only a few animals were permitted to be eaten and great care is to be taken to ease their suffering. Many people, both Jews and Gentiles alike, are aware of kashrut, or kosher, dietary laws. Kosher literally means "proper." Any food deemed kosher is permissible; non-kosher foods are treif. This translates from the word 'torn' and comes from Exodus 22:30 *Do not eat meat from an animal torn in the field.* Treif originally just referred to non-kosher meat, but over time came to include any food that wasn't proper.

Jews who observe Kashrut, which only encompasses 21% of American Jews,[7] will only eat mammals who chew their cud and have cloven hooves. Of sea creatures, only those who have fins and scales may be eaten. Birds of prey and scavenger birds may not be eaten, but chicken, ducks, geese and turkey are permitted. Insects, rodents, reptiles, and amphibians are all forbidden. All fruits and vegetables are permitted, with the exception of grape products. Those are only allowed if prepared by Jews.

However, it doesn't end there. Animals that can be eaten must be slaughtered in keeping with Jewish law. The animal has to be killed with a quick deep cut to the neck in order to minimize suffering. All the blood must be drained from the animal. The Torah is very clear on this; blood is life. Mixing meat and dairy is also prohibited. Exodus 34:26 *Do not cook a young goat in its mother's milk.* The segregation of meat and dairy extends to utensils, pots, pans, sinks, and dishwashers and care must be taken to keep them separate.

The Bible never explains why God permitted the consumption of certain meats after the world turned evil. Some Jews and Gentiles believe that it is primarily to keep the Jews healthy. And to be sure, pork and shellfish would be more dangerous in the era before modern stoves and refrigerators. However, candy and cookies can be kosher and very few people will claim that those are healthy foods. Others believe that it is to keep Jews a separate and holy people. Even the act of eating raises awareness and compassion. Rabbi Abraham Kook (1865-1935) was a firm believer that God's ideal diet for man was a vegetarian one. He thought that kosher laws were intended as a rebuke against those who lacked the moral self-control of a vegetarian diet. God intended the kosher laws to serve as a reminder that people should respect life, and that eventually, this would steer people back to His original, peaceful, plans. In his book, *A Vision of Vegetarianism and Peace,* Kook wrote:

It is impossible to imagine that the master of all that transpires, Who has mercy upon all His creatures, would establish an eternal decree such as this in the creation that He pronounced "exceedingly good," that it should be impossible for the human race to exist without violating its own moral instincts by shedding blood, be it even the blood of animals.

It is of interest to note, however, that although Rabbi Kook believed that God's original design called for mankind to follow a vegetarian diet, Kook himself was not vegetarian. Kook, and other prominent rabbis, believed that in the days of the Messiah mankind will return to the original vegetarian ideal. Rabbi Yitchak Abarbanel teaches that the peace in the Messianic Age extends to all creation. Evidence of this can be found in Isaiah 11 which teaches us the animals are no longer carnivorous. In the coming age, we will not only share paradise with the animals, but we will share our intellect and wisdom. Rabbi Rami Shapiro, based on texts from the prophets Isaiah, Joel, and Amos, believes that a worldwide return to vegetarianism may in fact hasten the arrival of the long awaited Messiah.

****

Muslims follow similar dietary customs. Food that is considered permissible is known as halal, while food that is forbidden is considered haram. Halal, while similar to Kashrut guidelines, are not as strict. Neither Jews nor Muslims may eat pork, carrion, insects, rodents, or blood. However, shellfish is permitted for Muslims. Both Muslims and Jews must cut the neck of the animal with a sharp blade and let all the blood drain out. The animal must not suffer needlessly. Beyond that, there are some minor differences. Since Halal regulations are not as rigid as kosher laws, a Muslim could eat kosher food and still be within Islamic laws, but a Jew may, in some cases, break kosher laws by eating halal food.

If an animal is halal, then the entire animal is considered permissible to eat. Conversely, if an animal is kosher, only the forequarter is kosher, the hindquarters are considered treif, as are the sciatic nerve and fat surrounding certain organs. All alcohol is forbidden according to the laws of halal, whereas Jews are allowed to consume alcohol as long as it conforms to other laws. Muslims who follow halal are permitted to mix meat and dairy. Despite common myth, kosher foods are not blessed by a rabbi, whereas Muslims always pronounce the name of Allah on each animal who is slaughtered.

To be considered Halal or Kosher, the animal must be slaughtered in a humane manner. The crux of the law is not only concerned with the treatment of the animal at the last moments of his life, but his whole life. Care must be taken throughout the life of the animal to ensure that he does not suffer needlessly. To be halal, the animals must be fed and watered before slaughter and they must not witness the slaughter of other animals. If an animal has been subject to abuse at any part of their life, up to and including slaughter, then their meat is considered haram. There is mild controversy in the west over Muslims who claim that factory farming renders all animals haram as they are kept in inhumane conditions throughout their lives.

Sufism, a belief and practice system in which its adherents try to find divine truth, has produced many vegetarians. These Sufis take literally Mohammad's admonishment to "not let your stomachs become graveyards." Many Sufis believe that vegetarianism is a key component in spiritual growth. 15th century poet Kabir believed that meat consumption was the failure of compassion and that those who ate animal flesh were deserving of eternal punishment. Instead of slaughtering animals, he taught that we should slaughter greed, attachment, lust, anger and pride.(8) Inayat Khan, a Sufi from the turn of the 20th century, believed that a vegetarian diet helps the purification of the body and refinement of the soul. Both Muslims and Jews believe that a vegetarian diet, while not required, can lead to greater spiritual attainment.

****

Christians, on the other hand, have no set of dietary laws comparable to kashrut or halal guidelines. Nevertheless, compassionate vegetarianism in Christianity is as old as the religion itself. St. James the Just, the brother of Jesus, was a vegetarian, as were many members of the early church. Historians Augustine and Hegisuppus make it a point to state that James was raised vegetarian. The Pauline letters hint at strife within the early church over whether it was proper to eat meat. Paul took a very pro-meat stance, calling vegetarians "weak" (Romans 14:2) but also writing that it shouldn't cause conflict. In 1 Corinthians 8:13 he writes that he wouldn't eat meat if it causes others to fall in faith. Clearly he believed that unity was more important than ethical dietary concerns. That he even bothered to mention it at all, and with such harsh language, shows what a real hot button issue it was within the early church.

The leaders of the early church: James, John, and Peter all followed strict vegetarian diets. As did Clement of Alexandria, Origen, Tertullian, John of Chrysostum, and many others. Not only did they not eat meat, but they taught ethical vegetarianism as the only way. The Early Jewish Christians, up into the 4th Century, followed this example and abstained from flesh. Throughout the ages, many saints were vegetarian. St. Jerome, 4th century theologian, and the first person to translate the Bible into Latin, once said "The eating of meat was unknown up to the big flood, but since the flood they have put the strings and stinking juices of animal meat into our mouths, just as they threw in front of the grumbling sensual people in the desert. Jesus Christ, who appeared when the time had been fulfilled, has again joined the end with the beginning, so that it is no longer allowed for us to eat animal meat."

In modern times, Christian vegetarians still crop up, but not with the frequency that was seen in the early church. John Wesley, the father of the Methodist movement was a vegetarian who boasted of improved health after he gave up meat and wine.(9) Wesley believed that a vegetarian diet was the only one compatible with Christian mercy. William Cowherd, founder of the Bible Christian Church, was a vegan who encouraged others to do likewise. Both Quakers and Seventh Day Adventists are Christian denominations who practice vegetarianism, and within the Holy Catholic Church, many monasteries practice it as well. Catholicism, though it condones meat-eating officially, has a long tradition of vegetarian saints, monks and nuns who believed that it was their moral duty to abstain from meat.

Some scholars argue whether Jesus himself was vegetarian. They believe that a meat-based diet was incompatible with His message of compassion and mercy. Others say that if James the Just was raised vegetarian then logically Jesus would have also been reared that way. Why on Earth would Mary make two separate meals if she didn't have to? Isaiah mentions the Messiah's diet consisting of honey and butter. Isaiah 7:15 *He will be eating curds and honey when he knows enough to reject the wrong and choose the right.* The historical Jesus was a Jew who followed Mosaic laws and Jewish customs. Jewish Christians in the early church followed Jesus' example. They differed greatly from the Gentile Christians that Paul converted who kept their western customs. Ultimately, The Pauline branch of Christianity won out and is what is practiced today. Without the proselytization of Paul it is likely that Christianity would be just another Jewish sect who continues to obey the Mosaic Laws.

Conversely, many other scholars maintain that Jesus ate meat. In Luke, Jesus is said to eat fish and many believe that since he celebrated Passover, it stands to reason that he ate the Passover lamb. Most Christians today take Paul's rebuke against vegetarians as proof that God intended for us to eat meat. Some feel so strongly that Jesus ate meat that they consider it sacrilegious to even suggest otherwise. At any rate, the Protestant and Catholic Bibles didn't say specifically what Jesus ate on any given day. Therefore, one must conclude that his diet was unremarkable. Unfortunately, for the topic of debate, that can be used as evidence for both sides depending on whether or not they view a meat-based or vegetarian diet as "normal".

Outside of niche groups, very few people spend much energy debating what Christ ate. Most people are happy to take a "live and let live" approach to modern religious vegetarianism. While it is not uncommon to find vegetarians within religious circles, they are still very much in the minority. Worldwide, vegetarians only number 375 million, out of a 7 billion world population.[10] of that 375 million, not all practice for religious reasons. Some do it out of environmental concerns or to live a healthy lifestyle.

Most vegetarians, however, do seem to be religiously and ethically motivated with Jains having the most vegetarians, Hindus coming in second, and Israeli Jews placing third. Though religious vegetarianism is a minority, it shows a desire for people to return to God's original vision. Even among meat eaters, you will find many who believe that God's vision of peace and harmony is the ideal. For diet is only a small part of the community God intended for his creation. It is worth noting, however, that of all the religions that recommend a vegetarian diet, only those who believe in the God of Abraham abstained exclusively out of recognition of God's loving concern for the animals, and the acknowledgement that we should do likewise.

****

A love of animals is wired into us all. We cheer for the Chicago Cubs, the Detroit Lions, and the Georgia Bulldogs. We read books about horses and cry over movies about dogs. We drive around in Mustangs and Thunderbirds while our children ride around on the brightly colored horses on the merry-go-round. Our favorite superheroes have the most noble characteristics of animals, possessing speed, agility, endurance, or strength. Animals pervade our pop culture and invade our homes. Two-thirds of all Americans share their living space with an animal; be it a dog, a cat, lizard, snake, bird, rabbit, rodent, or other. It's not merely a cultural phenomenon; throughout the history of the world people have bonded with animals. As humans we're social pack animals, but our companionship with animals goes far beyond that.

There is something inside all of us, whether or not we acknowledge it, that draws us to animals. We recognize a sameness in them, a spark, a like-mindedness, a spirit, or even a soul. We may take pride in our possessions. We may name our cars or own a treasured possession that has great intrinsic worth or sentimental value, but it's not the same. The tie that binds us to animals is different from that of humans, and drastically different from that of objects. We may be upset if we drop and break our cell phones. We may be concerned when our cars break down. But when our pets get sick or injured, we don't bemoan the inconvenience, we worry about our pets. We do what we can to make them better.

Surveys [11] show that married women believe their pets listen to them better than their husbands. A separate survey [12] has found that if we were to be stranded on an island for the rest of our lives with only one other being, most people surveyed would choose their pets over another human. This includes married couples and people with families. Our pets are the only companion that most people feel completely at ease around. They've seen us naked and not judged us. They've heard us sing and haven't complained. They've comforted us when we cry by crawling in our laps and licking our faces. With animals we let our guards down. We love them completely and unconditionally.

Our need for animal companionship is so strong that we spend billions on them annually and find ourselves accommodating them in ways we would never dream of doing for humans. Right this very minute a panic stricken woman is rushing her cat to the emergency vet. The bill will come to several hundred dollars and she will pay it without blinking an eye. As you are reading this sentence, a homeless man is sharing his only sandwich with his dog. Right now, a college student is spending $80 on flea prevention for her dog. She'll be living off of Ramen for the rest of the week. A father of four is spending half his paycheck to help his horse's injured leg. Every day people across the world are sacrificing something for the health and well-being of an animal. Where does this love for animals come from? It serves no evolutionary purpose.

If we are to take Genesis at face value, Adam and the animals were companions. They loafed around the Garden, enjoying fruits and nuts and communicating with one another. The Bible doesn't tell us how long this harmony lasted, but presumably all got along really well with one another or the Bible would have made it a point to state otherwise. The animals were all tame, God provided for everyone's needs, Adam didn't work, but spent every day by a flowing river, eating pomegranates, and relaxing with his animal friends under a shady tree. Eventually, the Bible doesn't say when, God decided that Adam needed a member of his own species to help him tend the Garden.

So He made Eve, and she and Adam and all the animals lived in harmony, with Adam and Eve being the designated caretakers of the animals and the Garden, as laid out in chapters 1 and 2. At this point in history life is perfect. No one works and all food is provided. Adam and Eve have nothing better to do than sit around all day playing and communicating with lions, foxes, rabbits, and squirrels, exactly as God had in mind when He created the universe. Life in the Garden was idyllic, and everyone lived in a peaceful utopia that God had deemed "very good."

Naturally, this harmony didn't last long. Satan, taking the form of a snake, talked Eve into eating the fruit of the Tree of Knowledge of Good and Evil. The Bible tells us that the snake *said to the woman "Did God really say 'you must not eat from any tree in the garden'?" The woman said to the serpent, "We may eat fruit from the trees in the Garden, but God did say, 'You must not eat fruit from the tree that is in the middle of the Garden."* The rest is history. Eve and Adam gained knowledge of the existence of evil; God in his wrath cursed the Earth, and future generations of humans lost out on paradise. Going backwards a couple of sentences, in order to trick Eve, the Bible tells us that the snake asked Eve a question and she calmly replied. She did not scream "Ahhh, a talking snake!" She merely answered his question, implying that it was an everyday occurrence.

If we are to take Genesis literally, we must accept that God allowed humans and animals to communicate. Now of course, the vocal ability of people and animals is quite a bit different. Even parrots who can literally speak to us in our own language, can't pronounce things exactly as we do. The vocal chords and tongues of most animals greatly differ from our own and they can't form vowels or consonants, and forget about lips. Some animals don't even have them. Good luck getting a chicken to say the letters "O" or "M." So they probably weren't speaking ancient Aramaic to each other, but they were able to communicate somehow. Interestingly, there has been research (see chapter 7) on primates to suggest that they use a rudimentary form of communication. Perhaps language isn't as unique to us as we previously thought. There's an old joke about how if dogs could talk they wouldn't be man's best friend. That wasn't the case in Eden, where everybody was happy and God was very pleased with His creation.

Not everyone believes Genesis to be a historical account, howbeit; some believe it to be an allegory. Tradition states that God handed down the story to Moses, but to what purpose? He had to have done it either as an account of world history or to tell a parable. The purpose of a parable is to teach a lesson in a way that was memorable to a preliterate or not-yet-fully literate society. If Genesis is an allegory the message does not change; God created the universe, God populated the universe with wondrous variety, God created people, God granted people free will, people messed up, now we live in a world of sin. God intended peace among all his creation, this remains true whether or not Eden is historical.

We know this because the books of Genesis and Isaiah both tell us that. This remains true regardless of how one interprets the tale of Adam and Eve. God envisioned a world of peace and love between people, between sexes, and between species. God didn't declare that the world was "very good" until He had made the entire world peaceful. God wanted the lion to lay down with the lamb and a little child to play with cobras. Deep down we all know how wonderful that would be. Animals and humans were no threat to each other. There were no predators, no prey, and no food chain. Originally there was to be no pain nor suffering for any species. That was the point of the opening chapters of Genesis, the rest is just details.

CHAPTER II

AFTER THE FALL

The fear of you and the dread of you shall be upon every beast of the Earth and upon every bird of the heavens, upon everything that creeps on the ground and all the fish of the sea.
Genesis 9:2

The Bible teaches that the entire world was vegetarian until the flood. In the first few chapters of Genesis, man and animal lived in harmony. Biblical researchers, dating from the time of creation until the flood using Biblical chronologies, place the time of the flood at 1656 Anno Mundi (1,656 years after the world was created). According to Genesis, prior to the flood, the patriarchs lived for centuries. Adam lived to be 930, his son Seth lived to 912, Methuseleh 969, and Enoch was taken to Heaven at 365 having never seen death. After the flood, the lifespan of humans dropped by 90%. Instead of living to be nearly one thousand, they were dying before they reached one hundred. As of this writing, the average lifespan worldwide is 71.4 years. [1]

Not everybody takes Genesis at face value. Even many devout Christians and Jews believe the stories of creation, paradise, and the flood to be allegories describing a larger point. Those who take a literal approach to Genesis believe that the difference in lifespans was due to genetic factors and the difference in cellular structures before and after the flood.

To be sure, if all humanity was wiped out save for eight people (Noah, his wife, their sons and daughters- in- law) that would certainly create a genetic bottleneck. Author and Researcher Bodie Hodge suggests an intriguing theory in support of this. (2) The Bible records Noah's death at the age of 950, but his son Shem was only six hundred when he died. Looking to the past, Lemech, Noah's father, was only 777 when he died. Compared to the rest of the population, he died young.

Hodge believes that Lemech carried a defective gene that was passed along to Shem, and later the rest of humanity. An interesting theory, but as with all theories on the subject, mere speculation. Nevertheless, it is worth noting that there is evidence that two historical bottlenecks happened that were significant enough to change human genetic diversity. (3) One took place around the Bering Strait, and the other in the Middle East/Africa region. There are many theories why this happened, from super volcanoes to disease, but as of yet, science isn't certain of the cause. It was, however, immense enough to alter the genetic diversity of humanity, especially when compared to the diversity found in other species.

Other people have come forward with theories ranging from the post-flood change in environments to the introduction of a meat-based diet. Of course, the latter is quickly ruled out. All vegetarians, including those who were vegetarian since birth, have approximately the same average lifespan as people who eat meat. Vegetarians living to be several centuries old would certainly be no secret today. The Bible, of course, never tells us why the lifespans decreased, only that it happened.

People who believe that an environmental change caused the drop in our lifespans believe that the pre-flood Earth was drastically different from the world we live in today. When God created the first humans they were physically perfect organisms in a perfect environment. Those who subscribe to this theory believe that the entire world was tropical, warm, and had richer oxygen. Citing the second chapter in Genesis, they believe that there was never any rain before the flood. Water vapor blanketed all the land creating a greenhouse effect. This vapor filtered dangerous radiation from the sun and increased longevity in humans. Worldwide, the climate was tropical, with no deserts, or ice caps. The topography was flat; valleys and mountains weren't created until after the deluge.

When God punished creation by sending a global flood, this canopy of vapor collapsed. For the first time water fell from the heavens and aided the development of the flood. After the flood, and without that canopy, cosmic radiation was first introduced into the world causing a drastic decrease in human lifespans. This theory, though interesting, does not explain why Noah's son still lived to be six hundred, despite living much of his life in a post flood world. Moreover, there is no evidence in the natural world to support this claim.

Antediluvian lifespans can be easily dismissed by the casual observer for lacking adequate scientific support. Many theories attempt to explain the phenomenon. One explanation is that ancient cultures had a different interpretation of what they considered a year. Perhaps a year to them involved a lunar orbit rather than a solar orbit. Saying that Methuseleh lived to be 969 months (which comes out to about eighty years) is a bit easier to digest than to believe he died just short of a millennium. Other theories suggest that a year was a season; therefore a child who was two years old by modern standards would have been eight by ancient interpretations.

Even just by looking at a modern calendar, we can see how things change, after all January and February are relatively recent months. When the original author wrote 'year' can we be certain they meant 365 days? Another take on it could be the numbering system itself. We assume that the numbers written were in base ten; positions of numbers are all to the 10th power so we have tens, hundreds, thousands, and so on. Problems arise however, when one fails to account for alternate number systems across cultures. Perhaps we are missing some data that would logically account for any discrepancies. The Bible was not written in modern English, it was written in ancient script, by and for people who had an intimate knowledge of their own culture.

Some researchers suggest the lifespans had a mystical meaning rather than a numerical value. We see a lot of symbolic numbers repeated in the Bible; why would we assume a literal meaning of outlandish longevity? It is worth noting, however, that the Biblical patriarchs aren't the only ones who are credited with hyper-longevity. Excavators discovered a stone tablet from ancient Mesopotamia that lists cities and kings from the ancient kingdom of Sumer, located in present day Iraq. This is known as the Sumerian King's List and provides valuable insight to the different monastic periods in Sumer and even has some astonishing parallels to Genesis. Sumer is the site of the earliest known civilization, and home to at least 12 city-states. Remarkably, the list mentions a "great flood" and names kings who ruled an average of 28,000 years. This makes the Biblical patriarchs seem like lightweights. After the flood, the reigns of kings settled into more realistic timeframes. Perhaps it was a common metaphor for that time period to ascribe unrealistically long life to important figures.

****

Whether or not you believe in a literal interpretation of early human longevity or even the great flood account, it is interesting to note that nearly every culture on Earth tells a story of a massive flood. There are over two hundred stories that involve such a catastrophe, and nearly all have the same refrain; a devastating deluge, a hero and his family who received advanced warning, a boat, local geography, and animals who play a key part in the story. The most famous and detailed flood myth, aside from the story of Noah and his family, is the Babylonian epic of Gilgamesh. This story has superficial similarities with the Noahic tale, including a wooden boat that eventually lands on a mountain. Both heroes send out a bird to find land, and both heroes save every animal yet offer one as a sacrifice.

Critics of the flood account believe that the story of Noah was copied from the Babylonian tale. However, this ignores the existence of a flood story in every ancient culture. It is unlikely, given the technology at the time, that they all copied the same source as some were from remote islands isolated from the rest of the world. The version taught to Muslims in the Quran is very similar to the Judaeo/Christian story of Noah, with some notable key differences. This should not be surprising as the Quran shares many elements of the Hebrew and Christian Bibles. In the Islamic version, the protagonist's name is Nuh (the Islamic word for Noah) and his wife and son were not spared, but other believers were; an indication that Allah is pleased by faith, not family connections. Additionally, there was no distinction between clean and unclean animals, and no sacrifice after the flood.

There is some debate among Islamic scholars about whether the flood was global or localized. Some claim it was regional and meant only to punish unbelievers who had been shown the way yet refused the truth, while others maintain that the waters engulfed the entire world. Those who believe in a worldwide deluge, however, are in a minority. Regardless, the moral of the story is that Allah meant to punish unbelievers, local or otherwise, and he accomplished this by way of a devastating flood. *He said: "Punishment and wrath have already come upon you from your Lord: dispute you have with me over names which you have devised- you and your fathers- without authority from Allah? Then wait: I am amongst you, also waiting." We saved him and those who adhered to him. By our mercy, and we cut off the roots of those who rejected our signs and did not believe.* (Quran 7.071-073).

As with the Judaeo/Christian account, and unlike a few other traditional accounts, the flood was sent exclusively to punish the wicked. In the tale of Noah, we have no indication of whether or not Noah tried to warn the populace ahead of time. By all accounts, the construction of the ark and the gathering of the animals took over 100 years, ample time to warn others. Genesis 18, details how Abraham pleaded and bargained with God to save the people of Sodom and Gomorrah, yet we have no indication that Noah did the same for the people of his time. In fact, Matthew 24:37-39, hints that the people had no warning, that they did not know what would happen until the flood came.

Does this mean that Noah didn't warn them, or that he did and they refused to listen? We have no record of it either way. In contrast, the Quran verse 7:63-64 states that Nuh tried to give advanced warning to the people so they could choose for themselves whether or not to be saved: *Do you wonder that there hath come to you a message from your Lord, through a man of your own people, to warn you, -so that you may fear Allah and happily receive mercy?" But they rejected him, and We delivered him, and those with him, in the Ark: but We overwhelmed in the flood those who rejected Our signs. They were indeed a blind people.* The flood was a punishment to unbelievers at the time of Nuh, and a warning and lesson to people in present times about the power of Allah's mercy and wrath.

****

In contrast to the Abrahamic versions, the Hindu flood myth is quite a bit different. This myth involves a king named Manu: the first man, father to all mankind, and the forerunner of all kings. While out washing his hands one day, he saw a small fish who begged Manu to save him. Manu placed the fish in a bowl, and as the fish rapidly grew, he eventually placed him in a tank. The fish quickly outgrew the tank as well, so Manu placed him in a small river, when the fish got too big for the river, Manu put him in the Ganges river, before finally releasing him into the ocean. When Manu released the fish into the ocean, he realized that the fish was Lord Vishnu who warned him that a catastrophic flood was imminent and promised to save him from it.

He instructed Manu to build a huge boat and take two of each kind of animal with him. Lord Vishnu, still in the form of a fish, towed the boat to the Himalayas where Manu would be safe from the deluge. Unlike the Noahic version, Manu was alone. When the waters receded animals repopulated the Earth, while Manu remained the sole human on a lonely planet. A year after the flood, a woman emerged from the depths of the sea, married Manu, bore his children, and the couple became the origin for all human life on Earth.

Through this myth we can see that Manu shares characteristics with both Noah and Adam. There are many other similarities and differences between the two legends. In the tale of Noah, God destroyed the world because it was wicked, whereas in Manu's story, the flood was just a natural event. Both men were saved through divine intervention, and both were saved by boats. Both save all the animals, start the new human race, and then both land on a known landmark; the Himalayas in Manu's account, and Mount Ararat in Noah's.

Recently, B.B. Lal, formerly of the Archeological Survey of India, found evidence that a real [4] flood did sweep away the Saraswati River, roughly some 4,000 years ago, giving credence to the story. Lal claims that the flooding was caused by a shift in tectonic plates. This obstructed the river's path and caused the subsequent flood and damage to the region. Since this took place at around the same time as the Manu account, Lal believes that this moves the legend from the realm of myth to history. While the flood itself has been proven, it is up to each individual to decide whether or not to believe the other details of the story.

****

The Buddhist version is markedly different from the legends found in other accounts. In this version, the flood is not global, but confined to an island. The Buddhist account is dated to the reign of King Brahmadatta, in Banares, India. There lay a city with a few thousand inhabitants and some corrupt carpenters. Among the carpenters were two leaders; one wise and one foolish. Each had a following of about five hundred people. The carpenters would accept payment and fail to deliver. Eventually the angry villagers ran them out of town. To escape they cut down trees, built a boat, and sailed down the Ganges River until they found a beautiful island in the middle of the ocean. This island was not without its inhabitants; there lived a wise man who warned them that the spirits who lived on the island hated filth. When the men defecated, they had to dig a hole to bury the waste so as not to enrage the spirits.

They obediently followed the instructions until one day they decided to throw a party. They made liquor from sugar cane and fell into drunken revelry. In their state of intoxication they relieved themselves everywhere and made no effort to clean it up. The spirits were furious and vowed to destroy the island and kill them all. However, one benevolent spirit felt the punishment was too harsh for the crime so he warned the carpenters to flee from the island. The wise leader took heed of the spirits warning and he and his followers built a great ship in which to escape. Meanwhile, the foolish leader and his men continued drinking, dancing, and polluting the island. One night, while the moon was full, massive waves crashed in from the ocean. The wise carpenter and his followers quickly clambered onto their boat and fled, while the foolish ones all drowned in the flood that swallowed the entire island.

This account varies greatly from the Genesis flood. In both stories the flood was sent as punishment and the protagonists escape by boat; however, no animals were spared in the Buddhist version and the flood was clearly a localized event. The moral of this story seems to teach wisdom and environmentalism. The reckless carpenters did not care for their island, so they lost it. The wise carpenters acknowledged their folly, heeded the warning of the spirits, fled and were saved. The foolish ones stayed and were drowned.

****

On the other side of the world in North America, the Ojibwe tribe have a flood myth that is not dissimilar to the Noahic tale. In this account, the world had turned evil and the creator, Kitch-Manitou, sent a flood to cleanse the Earth. When the flood came there was only one survivor, Nanabozho, who paddled around in a big canoe saving a pair of every animal. After floating around for a month, Nanabozo told the animals that he was going to swim to the bottom and collect some dirt to create some new land for them to live on.

Unfortunately, he was not able to reach the bottom. He then called the loon, and said "Since you are such a good swimmer, dive down to the bottom and bring some mud back in your bill." The loon dove down, and returned some time later with the report that the bottom was too far down, he couldn't reach it. So he sent the beaver to try next, to no avail. The animals argued over who would go next and the muskrat volunteered to try. He was ridiculed by the others, but managed to sneak out while they quarreled amongst themselves. After a long time had passed, the muskrat floated to the surface, a clump of mud in his hand, but at the cost of his life.

Kitch-Manitou allowed Nanabozho to breathe some life back into him. He then took the mud from the muskrat and shaped it into a ball. The ball grew and seeing that it needed a stand, the turtle offered his back. The ball continued to grow, and Nanabozho sent birds to fly around to see how big it was. The birds flew around and sent back their report through song, and to this day, birds will fly around and send the message on how the Earth is doing. Eventually, the ball of land was big enough to support life, and it is the planet we all live on today.

While the animals are anthropomorphized and play a greater role in this story, it shares a common backbone with the Biblical version of Noah. In both stories, an angry deity sent the water to cleanse the Earth from the evil that infected it. Both heroes, who were men of uncommon righteousness, float around on a wooden boat, saving the animals after a punishing flood. And both start the world over from scratch.

****

Proponents of the Genesis flood myth see the multiple accounts as evidence that there was a literal flood that covered the Earth and that other cultures adopted the Noahic account, revised it, and made it their own. Dr. John Morris, geological engineer and leading expert on the Biblical Flood, analyzed the flood myths (5) of two hundred cultures and found the following similarities:

- ✓ 88% Had a chosen family or hero.
- ✓ 66% Had advanced warning.
- ✓ 66% Of the floods were caused by man's evil.
- ✓ 95% Named the flood as the sole catastrophe.
- ✓ 95% The flood was a global rather than a local event.
- ✓ 70% Survived by boat.
- ✓ 67% Saved the animals.
- ✓ 73% The animals played an active role.
- ✓ 57% Survivors of the flood eventually land on a mountain.
- ✓ 82% Name local geography.
- ✓ 35% Involve birds being released.
- ✓ 75% Mention a rainbow.
- ✓ 3% Mention a sacrifice.
- ✓ 9% Exactly eight people were saved.

It is worth mentioning the 67% of myths that mentioned the heroes who saved the animals. What hidden spark is in us all that we put humanity into the guardianship role in these collective myths? Deep down we recognize that it's our duty to care for those weaker than us. We acknowledge that a world without animals is no world at all. The heroes in over half of all two hundred flood accounts went to a great deal of time and trouble to save our fellow animals because inside our collective consciousness's we understand God's command to take care of the Earth and all that is in it.

Maybe it's not so farfetched that every culture, including those who had no contact with other cultures, would have a flood myth. Until very recently boat was the best way to travel. Most civilizations sprang up around rivers and waterways, and we see truth of this even today; the most populous cities are still near water. Rivers and seas tend to rise and flood; in fact, many ancient civilizations counted on seasonal flooding to increase the fertility of their fields. So it should come as no surprise that they would have all eventually experienced a catastrophe so devastating that it would become its own legend. Can we absolutely rule out that it's not some collective memory of a common past event?

Scientists have found evidence of a massive flood in China (6) approximately 4000 years ago, the same estimated time as the Hindu flood. Recently, here in the west, Robert Ballard, whose team of underwater archeologists discovered the *Titanic* in 1985, took to the Black Sea in search of ancient civilizations. (7) Four hundred feet below the surface, he found just that. Evidence of an ancient shore, and proof of a catastrophic event around the same time as Noah's flood. Ballard believes that 150,000 square kilometers of land were washed away, and that this was the inspiration for the Biblical flood.

Nevertheless, it is worth noting that not all Americans believe the flood to be a physical historical account. In 2011, a Gallup poll (8) found that only:

> ✓ *27% Of Christians take the Bible to be the word of God to be taken literally.*

✓ *31% Find it to be the actual word of God, but with multiple possible interpretations.*

✓ *31% Believe it to be inspired by God, but not to be taken literally.*

✓ *7% See it as a book of fairy tales.*

✓ *4% Had no opinion on the subject.*

Many present- day Christians believe the flood to be based on a real-life local, rather than global, event and base their beliefs on both the archeological discoveries and on the Genesis 9:10 account where God makes His covenantal promise and appears to mention the animals on the ark separately from other animals: *I now establish my covenant with you....and with every living creature that was with you...all those that came out of the ark with you- every living creature on Earth.* Some believers interpret that as two separate groups of animals, while others believe it was the same.

Skeptics believe the idea of a literal flood to be preposterous. Some believe that we should take the lesson of the story, without attaching literal meaning to it. Others use the flood as an excuse to dismiss the entire Bible as ancient writers' works of fiction. After all, there are only seven basic storytelling plots in the world; overcoming the monster, the quest, rags to riches, comedy, tragedy, voyage and return, and rebirth. Why would a global flood not be one of them? It falls easily into the 'voyage and return" category of writing.

When reading the Bible, modern readers tend to study it using modern context. In general, this is a bad idea from the outset. One shouldn't view the past wearing modern lenses.

Cultures and situations are constantly in flux and it's a little too easy to get caught up in small details and miss the point of the larger picture. The past should be judged on its own merits and the present should focus on current sociological norms. It can be difficult for a modern reader to understand myths concerning global catastrophe, but such stories were common throughout ancient history.

With few exceptions, the majority of the current population understands that the Earth is round, the universe is vast, and that we have all sorts of equipment that can be used to measure and predict the weather. Ancient civilizations didn't have that luxury. They knew the four corners of their own world, and had their own ideas about the heavens and the rains. There were no satellites, Doppler Radars, modern maps, or other technological equipment that we take for granted. Geography and topography was different and has changed over the millennia. It is easy to believe that someone stuck on a boat with his family and livestock would see the devastation and assume that the entire world had been inundated...especially if their world only consisted of a few hundred miles or so.

One must also recognize the poetic device of words used in ancient stories. Is it so farfetched to believe that a writer, seeing the devastation and havoc wrought by a flood, would despair that their world was sunk? Is it beyond the realm of possibility that the words "world" and "land" could have been used interchangeably? While many people see the flood myth as a literary device to explain a larger narrative, there are those who take it as a literal, historical account. They believe that the layers of Earth that contain fossils were created by the flood, that the flood was the great extinction event that killed off the dinosaurs, and that the flood changed all the Earth's topography creating volcanoes and mountains.

The Bible is very clear on the details of the ark and flood. Would the original authors bother to include such details on mere fiction? The ark was specifically 450 feet long, 75 feet wide and 45 feet high. The authors specify that the ark was to be made of cypress wood and coated with pitch. There was to be a door on the side, and Noah had to make the boat three stories so there would be an upper, middle, and lower deck (Genesis 6:14-17). Skipping ahead, the Lord told Noah to *Go into the ark, you and your whole family...Take with you seven of every kind of clean animal, a male and his mate, and two of every kind of unclean animal, a male and his mate, and seven of every kind of bird, male and female to keep their various kinds alive throughout the Earth* (Genesis 7:1-3) in addition Noah was to bring along adequate food for himself, his family, and the animals.

Skeptics claim that a boat that size would collapse on itself and that the animals on the Earth wouldn't fit, would eat each other, or that Noah couldn't have physically collected animals from all around the Earth that he couldn't possibly have even known existed. Wooden boats aren't very practical; the largest ones in the modern era are only 300 feet long and leak even with reinforcements. Different animals have different needs. Present day keepers of exotic animals go through a great deal of time and expense to maintain a quality habitat for the animals to thrive. Everything from special UV lighting, hygrometers, humidifiers, dehumidifiers, heat lamps and an endless list of specialty products have to be purchased to care for such animals. Noah would not have had the means to care for animals with specialized diets, climates, and other needs.

Those who take the account literally claim that a boat that size could house every animal. After all, not every animal is the size of an elephant, a horse, or a cow. Hundreds of animals the size of rats, opossums, finches, or lizards could easily fit in the same room. They believe that for the larger land mammals, Noah could have brought along only the babies who would be considerably smaller. Keeping carnivores and herbivores separate wouldn't be an issue as the entire world was still vegetarian. Those who believe that some animals were carnivorous, believe that Noah brought along plenty of meat for them, and that the animals were housed separately so as not to have conflict. And of course, sea creatures, both large in size and numerous as they are, would need not be housed on the ark. Sea life did not get a free pass, howbeit, as many would have died when the waters receded.

****

Whether you view the flood as an historical event or an instructive, cautionary tale, we need to be careful to still observe the forest among the trees. The story, passed down orally for generations before, eventually written and preserved for thousands of years, was not without cause. What is the moral of the story? From the time of creation until the time of the flood, mankind had fallen so far from God's original plan that he felt the need to start over. Paradise, our communion with God, nature, and animals, had changed forever. That is the crux of the story; everything else is mere detail. Mankind had already fallen and turned wicked. Paradise was lost; man had lost his relationship with God, his stewardship over nature, and his community with animals. Noah was said to have been the most righteous of his generation. Just how evil was his generation? Would Noah be considered more holy by today's standards, or less? Unlike other Biblical heroes, no good deeds are mentioned in association with him aside from the ark. We only know that he was "perfect in his generation" (Genesis 6:9).

From the time of Adam to the time of Noah, we actually know very little. If the Biblical timeline is to be taken literally, a little more than 1,600 years had passed. However, that timeframe is based on a Biblical family tree. It is entirely possible that only the most important figures were named. If this is the case, then hundreds or even thousands of years could have passed between the named patriarchs. This would make the timeline between Adam and Noah much longer.

Whatever that timeframe may be, it takes place between two chapters; Genesis 3 marks the fall of man and Genesis 5 tells of the birth of Noah. From a historical perspective, this is nothing more than a blink of the eye. In the course of millions and billions of years, what's a millennium? Nevertheless, a lot can happen in that time period, and we know very little of what did. All the Bible tells us is that man was very wicked and that "every inclination of the thoughts of his heart was only evil all the time." There was anarchy; no religious leaders to guide the way, no monarchs to call for order, no divine moral code, no religion or law whatsoever. One can only imagine what great evil took place that would prompt such regret and destruction.

God had instructed man through Adam to rule the Earth. Unfortunately, Adam had fallen and proved himself unworthy of the task. It is no accident that God instructed Noah to save the animals. God could have destroyed mankind without harming a single animal. Or he could have saved a select few by other means; instead he had Noah go to a great deal of time and expense to save a sample of every species. Noah and his family were forced into a caregiving role. The same role that Adam and Eve were instructed, but ultimately failed to take on.

Anyone who has ever been owned by a pet knows that they take a great deal of time and attention to care for. If a person has one cat, for example, they have to feed and water the cat and change the litter box. If a person has a dog, they have to feed, water, and walk him. The more pets a person has, the more work involved. The eight people on the ark would have been consumed with animal care, day in and day out. There would have been no break from the constant chores. That was the price they had to pay to live. The entirety of the whole animal kingdom rested on the shoulders of Noah and his family. If they failed, an entire species would be wiped out. That's no small responsibility. In Eden, Adam and Eve were responsible for the welfare of all creation. In an act of disobedience they lost their place in paradise, but they were never relieved of the role of caretaker.

When many people ask about the flood, the first thing they ask about are the animals. Much of it is the usual questions; what did they eat? How did they all fit? How did they come from different climates and meet in the Middle East? Et cetera. Another common question is 'why did God kill all the animals?' By instructing Noah to build the ark and provide adequate food for all the animals, God is often credited as being merciful. He provided a way for them to escape mass extinction. He personally communicated with the animals to lead them to the ark. Some believers view this as an act of mercy; other believers view this as the ultimate cruelty. God saw fit to destroy mankind for their sins, but why punish innocent animals?

****

Some people believe that during this timeframe the Earth was in such spiritual decay that the animals had become corrupt as well. The earliest humans were to rule over the Earth in the same manner a benevolent king rules his subjects: with kindness, grace, and mercy. Mankind, according to this theory, corrupted both himself and animals, flaunting the role of guardian. Because people were so corrupt, the Bible tells us they were wicked from birth, they dragged the animals down to their level of moral decay. Theophilus, Bishop of Antioch during the 2nd century certainly believed this theory. He felt that when man fell from Grace the animals fell with him, and that if people could turn from evil and rise to their original level of goodness, then the animals would follow them back to their original gentle nature.

This isn't outside of the realm of possibility; animals do have a spiritual side. The Psalmists call for every living thing to worship the name of the Lord. Psalm 148 sings of all of creation singing praise for the Lord, from the sea creatures in the depths, to the wild and domestic animals, to the small creatures, to the birds in the air. Psalm 150 calls on everything that has breath to praise the Lord. In the New Testament, in Matthew 8:28-34 there is further support for animal spirituality, when we learn that on one occasion Jesus drove out evil spirits and sent them into animals.

When he arrived at the other side of the region of the Gadarenes, two demon-possessed men coming from the tombs met him. They were so violent that no one could pass that way. "What do you want with us, Son of God?" they shouted. "Have you come here to torture us before the appointed time?" Some distance from them a large herd of pigs was feeding. The demons begged Jesus, "if you drive us out, send us into that herd of pigs." He [Jesus] said to them "Go!" So they came out and went into the pigs, and the whole herd rushed down the steep bank into the lake and died in the water. Those tending the pigs ran off, went into town and reported all of this, including what had happened to the demon possessed men.

We learn a bit about animal spirituality from this. The demons attack the pigs, they don't get sent into the mountains or the lake; they chose to enter into the animals. It was their idea, not Jesus' idea, and certainly not the pigs. Furthermore, this transfer would not be possible if the animals lacked a soul. Because they had souls the pigs were a target, but the tale doesn't end there, this story has many layers. The pigs rushed down the mountain, into the water and drowned. Pigs are quite capable of swimming.

We know the demons didn't cause the pigs to drown, a sentence earlier, they begged Jesus to save them. Jesus didn't cause the pigs to drown. The pigs either chose to commit suicide rather than live with an evil spirit, or they were so panicked by the demons that they lost their senses. The pigs were an unfortunate casualty in a cosmic war outside their control. Of all the accounts of Jesus and his disciples casting out demons, this is the only one where they possess another soul, be it a human or animal soul. As far as we know, this is the only instance in history of demons begging to be transferred.

The pigs showed us that they would rather die than live with demon possession. The two possessed humans didn't make that decision. Does this suggest the pigs had greater morality? Moreover, Matthew tells us that both Jesus and the spirits knew that it was not the demons time to die. By entering the pigs the demons were able to bring immediate destruction to the swine herder, thereby maximizing their havoc. No one foresaw the actions of the pigs; they were a wildcard and acted of their own volition.

Yet another layer of the story is the status of pigs to the Hebrew culture. Jesus said that he came to fulfill the law, not abolish it, we see many examples of this, and here we see it in the idea of clean and unclean animals. Perhaps there is a moral connection to the idea of even 'unclean' pigs being unwilling to live with a demon. Could this suggest a higher moral conscience for the pigs than for the men who were originally possessed? Of course, we'll never know the answer to these questions.

This isn't the only Biblical story where we get to see the spiritual side of animals, who with their free will throw a wrench into the plans of men and God. Balaam's donkey is yet another example. Numbers 22 tells of Balaam, a prophet who was not right with the Lord. He was summoned by Balak, King of the Moabites, to curse the Israelites. After Balaam initially turned down Balak's offer, he eventually agreed to meet with him. Balaam saddled his donkey and rode out to meet the King Balak, a move that angered God.

God sent an angel to thwart the efforts of Balaam. The donkey saw the angel standing in the middle of the road and turned into a field to avoid him. Balaam, angry, beat the poor donkey to get her back on the road. The angel then moved to a path with two vineyards, surrounded on both sides by a wall. Once more, the donkey moved to avoid the angel, crushing Balaam's foot in the process. As a result, he beat her once again. Finally, the angel moved to a narrower place where the donkey could not turn. Rather than pass the angel, the poor girl lay down on the road. This time Balaam beat her with his staff.

This leads to one of the more bizarre tales in the Bible; the Lord miraculously allows the donkey to speak. Through a miracle of God, this donkey was able to vocalize her thoughts in a way that Balaam understood. "What have I done to you to make you beat me these three times?" She asks. Balaam, not pausing to wonder why an animal was speaking to him, yells at her that she made a fool of him, saying that he would have killed her if he'd had his sword. The donkey then asks Balaam if she'd been in the habit of disobedience, to which he was forced to answer "no."

It is only then that God opened Balaam's eyes and allowed him to see the angel. The angel rebukes Balaam asking why he beat the poor girl and informing him that were it not for the donkey he would have killed Balaam, but spared the donkey. The angel's original intent was to kill Balaam, who had no idea the angel was even there. The angel, who was plainly seen by the donkey, had his mission interrupted. Good did come of this, Balaam ended up cursing Balaak, but were it not for his spiritually-attuned beast of burden; he would have died out there on the road.

This story, and the one in Matthew about the pigs, show us that animals are one with the spiritual side of life. Both the pigs and the donkey acted of their own free will and behaved in ways that God had not planned. The former by their mass suicide, and the latter by turning away from the angel in the road. This spirituality is no surprise to the authors of the Bible who spoke often of the spiritual side to animals in the Book of Psalms, and the books of Job, Ezekiel, and others.

Nor would it surprise Charles Darwin who believed that we got our spiritual side from the animals, or Jane Goodall, who also believes that animals evidence a form of spirituality. So perhaps there is truth to the theory that man's corruption after the fall also corrupted the spiritual lives of animals. After all, if they can be spiritually good, then it stands to reason that they can be spiritually bad as well. To those who believe this theory, God was punishing *all* the wicked of the Earth and only the most moral of the humans and animals were spared from the flood.

****

As with much to do with the flood, the spiritual fallibility of animals is mere Biblical speculation. We do not know how animals behaved, or how people treated the animals during the antediluvian time period. God had instructed a vegetarian diet; however, man had already broken God's singular law regarding the Tree of Life. God intended harmony, but we lost this during the fall. Did mankind eat animals during this time frame? We may have reason to believe that they did. Adam's son Abel kept flocks. For what reason would he have kept them if not for consumption or the use of wool? They definitely weren't pets; it seems as if by the second generation of humans we were already exploiting animals.

Did people corrupt animals, or were they innocent? Were people cruel to them or gentle? It would be easy to imagine that they treated animals with the same cruel regard and indifference that they treated each other, but we have no proof of that. All we know is that God saw fit to ensure the survival of the animal species. Man's wickedness was so immense that God was sorry he ever created humans, yet He still created a window for their salvation; a similar theme to the birth, death, and resurrection of Jesus.

In Eden there were no rules save one: do not eat from the tree of knowledge of good and evil. Obviously, Adam and Eve broke that rule, gained awareness of the existence of evil and life descended into moral decay. The flood teaches us that man had fallen into such ruin that God felt it necessary to destroy everything and start fresh. The first couple of chapters in Genesis tell us how pleased God was with creation, and the hopes he had for the success of mankind. Early man did not live up to those ideals. Whereas Eden had only one rule, when God wiped out the Earth to begin anew, he added new rules that all of mankind was to follow.

These are known as the Noachide laws. Because Noah is credited with being the new father of humanity, these laws apply to all people, in contrast to the Mosaic laws, which applied only to the Israelites. In this new world, as a concession to the violence in human nature, God granted that man could now eat animals. But this concession came at a price, Genesis 9:2 warns that now the animals will fear people: *The fear and dread of you will fall upon all the beasts of the Earth, and all the birds of the air, upon every creature that moves along the ground, and upon all the fish of the sea.*

God granted Adam dominion over animals in Genesis 1 and 2. The dominion that we have over animals is not dissimilar to the dominion a parent has over their child. In Genesis 9, that dominion was replaced with fear. In Eden mankind had fellowship with the animals; in this new world we lost that harmony. What a terrible price we pay to sin.

CHAPTER III

THE COVENANT

I now establish my covenant with you and with your descendants after you and with every living creature that was with you- the birds, the livestock, and all the wild animals, all those that came out of the ark with you-every living creature on Earth.
Genesis 9:9-10

After the flood, God promised Noah that He would not destroy the Earth again because of man, "*even though every inclination of his heart is evil from childhood. And never again will I destroy all living creatures as I have done.*" (*Genesis 8:21*) Previously, God had destroyed the Earth because of man's wickedness, but now He seems to have made peace with it. Whether you take the flood account literally or as a cautionary tale, here Noah's life mimics Adam's. By the time he had emerged from the ark, vegetation had begun to grow again. It was just Noah, his family, and the animals left on Earth. Only now, the animals fear humans; the previous community with them is gone. Genesis 1:28 and Genesis 9:1 both quote God's blessings on Noah and on Adam: *Be fruitful and increase in number and fill the Earth*. But where God followed the blessing by telling Adam to rule over the Earth, He told Noah that the creatures of the Earth would now fear him. Our relationship had forever been altered.

We lost out on paradise, but the fall of man and the flood are written in the first book of the Bible, not the last. Though we lost our original communion with nature, God still had a plan for us all. Not only did God bless Noah and his family after the flood, He made a promise to them, and He made it a point that this promise would extend to all life on Earth. God vowed that never again would He destroy the entire Earth by flood.

As a sign of that promise, He made a rainbow appear in the sky. If the flood was indeed a global historical account, then this would have been the first rainbow to ever appear on Earth. Before the flood the atmosphere was too different from our current one to support a rainbow. (See the antediluvian theories in chapter 2.) God wanted that physical sign to signify His promise to all life on Earth. The rainbow was God's symbol of his covenant. Humans have adopted another symbol from this story, this one to represent peace: the dove holding an olive branch. This is noteworthy, as it combines nature, animals, and humans working together, adding yet another parallel to the Noah and Adam accounts.

When God created the universe, He didn't make humanity the center. Astronomy tells us that there is no center. God created the universe and He made it wondrous. He created the world in its entire verdant splendor. He made life with variety beyond comprehension; insectivorous plants, pilot fish, living great barrier reefs, kangaroos, opossums, hippopotamuses, duckbilled platypuses; the list is endless. The Bible tells us that God created animals for His pleasure and He delights in them. Our original communion with the animals, and the dominion we had over them were part of God's blessing. In Genesis, we are told that creation was "very good." In chapter 104:24-28 the Psalmist sings praise to God's care for His creation.

How many are your works, O Lord! In wisdom you made them all; the Earth is full of your creatures. There is the sea, vast and spacious, teeming with creatures beyond number- living things both large and small. There the ships go to and fro, and the leviathan, which you formed to frolic there. These all look to you to give them their food at the proper time. When you give it to them, they gather it up; when you open your hand they are satisfied with good things. And in verse 31 *may the glory of the Lord endure forever; may the Lord rejoice in His works.*

God did not just wind up the world like a top and watch it spin. He takes a vested interest in His entire creation, from the tiniest mammal that scampers across the Earth to the largest whale in the ocean. God blessed both humans and animals with the capacity to love life. The 104th psalm, verse 26 says that the leviathan (most likely a whale) "frolics" in the sea. The book of Job speaks often of God's care for creation and their zest for life. Job 39:13 says "the ostrich spreads her feathers to run and laughs at the horse and rider." Chapter 40 speaks of the behemoth (possibly a hippopotamus or an elephant), who eats from hills filled with food while wild animals play nearby. God makes it a point to tell Job that the behemoth was created alongside man; by the same creator, and presumably for the same reason.

In Ecclesiastes 3:18-20, Solomon equates human life with animal life. *I also thought, "As for men, God tests them so that they may see they are like the animals. Man's fate is like that of the animals; the same fate awaits them both. As one dies, so dies the other. All have the same spirit; man has no advantage over the animal. Everything is meaningless.* God created man and animal with the intent that they play and have fun. The text in Ecclesiastes is melancholy, but surrounding verses say that there is nothing better for man than to eat, drink, be happy and do good, for our lot in life is the same as the animals. In Genesis man disobeyed God; His punishment is that we now have to work for food. Genesis 3:14 says that man is now cursed above all the animals, both domestic and wild. While the animals rely on God for every goodness, we humans have to sweat for it.

****

God created animals for His sake and His delight; it only stands to reason that His plans would include them. As humans we tend to see the fact that God made covenants with us as proof that we hold an exalted place in the universe, but the Bible doesn't support that. God's pledge is with all living creatures, and will remain in effect for as long as the Earth remains. God could have just made His covenant with the animals and never told us about it, but God wanted us to know. Five times Genesis 9 repeats this promise:

"I now establish my covenant with you and with your descendants after you and with every living creature that was with you – the birds, the livestock and all the wild animals, all those that came out of the ark with you – every living creature on Earth. I establish my covenant with you: Never again will all life be cut off by the waters of a flood; never again will there be a flood to destroy the Earth."

And verse 12 reads *And God said "This is the sign of the covenant I am making between me and you and every living creature with you, a covenant for all generations to come."*

Verse 15 again mentions it, *I will remember my covenant with me and you and all living creatures of every kind.*

Verse 16-17; *whenever a rainbow appears in the clouds, I will see it and remember the everlasting covenant between God and all living creatures of every kind on the Earth." So God said to Noah, "This is the sign of the covenant I have established between me and all life on Earth."*

It may seem redundant that the same basic sentence is repeated so often in the same chapter, but to the sages and rabbis who believe that God does not waste words, it emphasizes that God's promise encompasses all life and not just one species. It is no accident that this covenant comes after the verses about eating meat and the fear animals will now have of humans. If God felt no concern for His animals, why would He include them in His contract? He repeats this promise so many times because He wants to make absolutely sure we know that they are included. The repetition signifies the immense importance of His words. He would not have bothered to do that if they held no special place for Him.

In Genesis 9:2 God proclaims that the animals will fear us, this is a curse to all animals and humans. Luckily, this was not God's final word on the subject. The book of Hosea 2:18 states: *In that day I will make a covenant for them with the beasts of the field, the birds in the sky and the creatures that move along the ground. Bow and sword and battle I will abolish from the land, so that all may lie down in safety.* It is a tragic truth that humans kill animals at an exponential and unsustainable rate, but it would be a lie to pretend that humans are safe from animals.

Ranging from ants and bees which kill approximately three dozen people per year, to elephants [1] who kill hundreds, crocodiles and scorpions who kill thousands, and the most deadly animal of all; mosquitoes who kill millions, neither animals nor humans are safe from one another. We learn from Genesis and the prophets that this relationship is not God's ideal. After Adam and Eve ate from the fruit and lost their innocence, their relationship with the natural world was cursed. Man had to toil the fields, women experienced painful childbirth, and humans and animals became enemies; Genesis 3:15 God told the serpent *they shall strike at your head and you shall strike at their heel.* Hosea 2 is a reminder that one day we will no longer live together in such discord.

The book of Hosea is not a cheerful one. It is an analogy about the love of God for His 'adulterous' people. The prophet Hosea married a prostitute and felt grief when she stepped out on him, at one point going so far as to sell herself into slavery. Hosea, still in love, bought her back. This book is symbolic of God's love for His chosen people; though they stray, He takes them back. The second chapter is all about the punishment and restoration of mankind in general, and the Israelites in particular. It is a reminder that all of creation, humans and animals, will live once again in harmony and unity with God, with no violence, no bloodshed, and no fear. Though things look bleak in the present, the curse will one day be lifted and we can look forward to the future that we will experience together.

This passage, along with Isaiah 11 and 65 (as we saw in chapter 1), emphasizes the new heaven and Earth. Animals and humans will live in peace on God's Holy Mountain. There will be no death or bloodshed; there will be no more pain or fear. By no means is Isaiah the only Biblical prophecy to include the welfare of animals and the harmony with which we all live. Joel 2:21-23 tells us to *Be not afraid, O land; be glad and rejoice. Be not afraid, O wild animals, for the open pastures are becoming green. The trees are bearing their fruit; the fig tree and the vine yield their riches. Be glad, O people of Zion, rejoice in the Lord your God, for he has given you a teacher for righteousness. He sends you abundant showers, both autumn and spring rains as before.*

Here is yet another prophecy that promises peace and comfort for all creation. The land can rejoice, the animals can relax and eat their fill, and the people can enjoy rest in righteousness. Notice the list Joel used; he went in ascending order, the same order God used when creating the earth. There is a special point, howbeit for people; God has given us a teacher for righteousness (whom Christians believe to be Jesus Christ). In Eden we had no such provision and we fell hard. In the new world, we won't repeat the same mistake.

****

Animals, as fellow citizens of the world, are often included as a matter of fact for punishment, redemption, and even salvation. In the previous chapter we learned how the animals were punished in the great flood, but alongside Noah and his family a few were spared. The book of Jonah speaks of another prophet and his warning of disaster to the people of Nineveh. Nineveh, the capital of Assyria, was located on the banks of the Tigris River, in present-day Mosul, Iraq. It was a magnificent city with gardens, public parks, temples, huge palaces, aqueducts and canals. It also had a library which was home to over 30,000 inscribed clay tablets. [2]

Archeology tells us it was a huge metropolis, and the Bible tells us it was as wicked as it was grand. The Biblical book of Nahum describes a cruel, bloodthirsty people. Archeological records support this view. (3) The pictures and inscriptions that have been left for us in the form of cylinders, tablets, and prisms describe a gory scene and ruthless leaders. Soldiers dismembered captives, rebels were flayed and staked, and ruler Sennacherib was even murdered by his own sons, who were as wicked and bloodthirsty as he.

No, the Assyrians were not nice people, so God had plans to destroy the entire city. The Israelites hated the people of Nineveh, but God's mercy extends to all. He sent Jonah to warn the people of their impending doom. Jonah, son of Amittai, was a prophet between the years 786-746 BCE, during the reign of King Jeroboam II. In a story that is familiar to Jews and Christians, when God sent him to warn Nineveh, Jonah fled. Forgiveness may be divine, but Jonah, though a prophet was still human after all, and he wanted the city destroyed.

The book of Jonah tells us that while he was fleeing, he was swallowed up by a great fish, chapter 1:17 *But the Lord provided a great fish to swallow Jonah, and Jonah was inside the fish three days and three nights.* Interpreters differ on whether or not the story is a parable, or an actual event. There are historical records from the 19th century of whales biting sailors or dragging them into the water only to spit them back out again. The Bible never says that Jonah was inside the fish's stomach (which would be filled with stomach acids), only that he was inside him. Is it beyond belief that he stayed inside the mouth of a whale for three days? This wouldn't be the first time God used an animal to accomplish

ON THE FIFTH DAY

His goal. Or perhaps, the fish was no earthly creature, but a heavenly being sent down by God to secure Jonah and bring him safely to dry land.

On the other hand, there are scholars, researchers, and ministers who believe the story to be a parable, intended to narrate a larger point. Whether you believe the story to be a parable or a historical narration, its purpose is to describe God's love and patience. Jonah ran from God and was saved and forgiven. Once in Nineveh he warned them of God's wrath and impending punishment. The Ninevites believed God, and as Jonah feared, they repented. Jonah 3:6-9:

When the news reached the king of Nineveh, he rose from his throne, took off his royal robes, covered himself with sackcloth and sat down in the dust. Then he issued a proclamation in Nineveh: "By the decree of the King and his nobles: Do not let any man or beast, herd or flock, taste anything; do not let them eat or drink. But let man and beast be covered in sackcloth. Let everyone call urgently on God. Let them give up their evil ways and violence. Who knows? God may yet relent and with compassion turn from his fierce anger so that we will not perish."

The king of Nineveh made it a point to include the animals in his decree. They were to take part in the fasting and wear sackcloth along with the rest of the city. It sounds silly for a ruler to demand fasting and repentance from an animal, but so great was the king's fear that he wanted all the inhabitants of the city to repent. The story doesn't end here. Verse 10 tells us that God had compassion and turned from His wrath. This angered Jonah who wanted the city destroyed; he complained to God that it was better to die than to live. Jonah went east of the city to sulk; he made shelter and watched Nineveh. God caused a vine to grow up out of the ground and provide shade, which pleased Jonah, but at dawn God destroyed the vine. Once again, a bitter Jonah complained to God saying "It would be better for me to die than to live." Jonah 4:9-11:

But God said to Jonah, "Do you have a right to be angry about this vine?"

"I do," he said "I am angry enough to die."

But the Lord said, "You have been concerned about this vine, though you did not tend it or make it grow. It sprang up overnight and died overnight. But Nineveh has more than a hundred and twenty thousand people who cannot tell their right hand from their left, and many cattle as well. Should I not be concerned about that great city?"

Once again animals are named alongside the humans. In a catastrophe, all the animals in the city would be casualties in the war against good and evil. God did not say He only cared about the human inhabitants; rather He made it a point to include the animals in His statement of mercy. It is also curious that the king included animals in his decree for penance. If anything, it's evidence of how seriously he took Jonah's warning; he took no chances. Now obviously, he couldn't control the actions of the wild animals. Though he did mention them, and he held the domestic animals and livestock in high enough regard that he felt the need to use them to cover all his bases. At any rate, it worked; the Bible is clear that his act of repentance was successful. And who knows? Perhaps God made it a point to mention that the cattle had been spared because the king went to such lengths to include them in his decree.

It is worth noting that Nineveh, indeed all of Assyria, was eventually destroyed in 612 BCE. The books of Nahum and

Zephaniah predict her eventual downfall. Nahum predicts that other nations will clap their hands at her eventual ruin, as all have felt the city's merciless cruelty. Interestingly, it seems as though God spared the animals after all. Chapter 2:14 predicted that flocks and herds and animals of every kind will use the ruins of the city as their homes, and owls will use the city's once great columns to roost.

****

The story of Ninevah wasn't the first time animals were potential casualties of divine punishment. After the Israelites left Egypt they went to the Promised Land, a trip that took forty years to complete. There are many reasons why it took so long. The Bible tells us that the original Jews grumbled so much against God that He wasn't going to let them see the "land flowing with milk and honey." A theory among some scholars is that in addition to the punishment against those who challenged God's authority, the slave mentality of the Israelites had to die out. It was a new generation who saw the Promised Land. Not those who suffered under the Pharaoh in Egypt. Another reason for the wait was Jericho's current inhabitants; God is not one to punish innocent people. The Jerichites were already on a dangerous downward trajectory. They soon reached the epoch of wickedness; child sacrifice, bestiality, idolatry, and violence were common practices throughout the city. Only when there was no one left to be saved, were the Israelites able to enter and claim victory.

Jericho, located on the West Bank of Israel, is one of the oldest continually inhabited settlements in the world. It dates back to about 9000 BCE and has been very archaeologically important to researchers as they have traced humanities' first stages of civilization. (4) Archeologists have been able to find evidence of a town during the period that the settlement was destroyed by God and the Israelites. Unfortunately, erosion and time have worn down the city enough that we can't pin down an exact date. Nevertheless, we do know that Jericho was destroyed, and the Bible tells us that it was due to the evil ways of the populace.

Joshua 6:20 gives account of the destruction. *When the trumpets sounded, the people shouted, and at the sound of the trumpet, when the people gave a loud shout, the wall collapsed; so every man charged straight in, and they took the city. They devoted the city to the Lord and destroyed with the sword every living thing in it- men and women, young and old, cattle, sheep, and donkeys.* (Joshua 6:20-21) We see, once more, that the animals were not spared; the entire city was laid waste as surely as if an atomic bomb had been dropped.

Total destruction of human and domestic animals was the price they paid for their evil acts. Tending livestock in various capacities was a common occupation throughout history. While on the surface it may seem that destroying the Jerichites livelihood was equivalent to rioters looting businesses, or warlords burning fields, the Israelites goal was to kill all the inhabitants of Jericho. Destroying somebody's job is pointless if you've already killed that person. The Israelites were told to kill all citizens, and to them, that meant the animals as well.

****

Animals are often included in tales of punishment in the Bible and in history. This makes sense; humans don't live in a vacuum. When modern countries drop bombs on cities, those bombs destroy everything; soldiers, civilians, children, and the elderly, along with pets, livestock, wildlife, and even the natural world. Parts of Europe are still carved up from World War I. Even the act of war itself is brutal for animals.

Animals from camels, to donkeys, horses, elephants, dogs, and even pigeons have all been placed on the frontline and been killed by arrows, cannons, guns, and bombs. Many species of animals to this day have received medals and recognition for their part in wars. In the First World War, horses were fitted with gas masks to protect them from chemical warfare. Of course, this ultimately didn't save them from other dangers. In a war that killed ten million humans, it took the lives of eight million horses.[5] The number of total animals killed in that single war is lost to history, though some estimates total over nine million.

Tens of thousands of Pigeons were used during the First World War to relay important messages. One pigeon, Cher Ami, saved nearly two hundred soldiers before being killed by German bullets. Another pigeon, "The Mocker," was wounded and retired after flying fifty-two missions.[6] Homing pigeons were killed by guns, falcons, and hawks. Along with pigeons, dogs were also on the frontline. The most famous, Sergeant Stubby was a pit bull who witnessed seventeen major battles in just a year and a half. Stubby was trained to sniff mustard gas and warned of incoming missiles. He returned from the war a hero, having received more medals than most people, and he even got to meet the president. Stubby died a natural death in 1926.

Animals in combat weren't the only casualties of war. Just as innocent civilians lose their lives, so too, do their pets and livestock. Between the bombing of cities, starvation, and disease, many animals die alongside their humans. Families lose beloved pets and wild animals are killed in the crossfire. It is a lucky soul who escapes unscathed.

War is hell.

Tragically, some animals are intentionally killed. At the outbreak of WWII, and with the memory of the first Great War still heavy on everyone's minds, the British government sent out pamphlets and left notices in newspapers calling for the people to kill their pets. The rationale behind such an extreme proclamation was that it was kinder to kill them than to release them to roam or let them starve. It was a drastic step, but people panic at the thought of war. In the first week alone, as many as 750,000 (7) pets were killed. Sadly, such acts were not uncommon. Throughout the ages pets, livestock, and other animals have been taken by the cruel hands of war.

****

The important thing to remember is that death and destruction were never part of God's original design. We were all punished in the fall, and we all suffer together. God intended for man to guide and care for animals in the same way He does. We can see this in Genesis 2:15 where He said exactly that: *The Lord God took the Man* (Adam) *and put him in the Garden of Eden to work and take care of it.* We can also see that in the promises God made in Genesis 9 and in Hosea 2. This inclusive covenant is unique to the Judaeo/Christian faiths, none of the other major religions boast of such a promise between a deity and animals.

Though compassion towards animals is encouraged by all religions, none other than the Jewish and Christian religions mention a covenant between a god or gods and animals, and none save for the Abrahamic faith's speak of a god's love and joy for the animals. Buddhists, Jains, and Hindus will often depict gods as animals. They also believe that animals have souls that are roughly on par with that of a human. Yet none of them believe that a god takes a vested interest in the lives of animals and none mention a sheer, unbridled joy such as that the God of Abraham takes in His creation. It turns out a creator big enough and powerful enough to create an entire universe *ex nihilo* is big enough and powerful enough to love all living things. Who knew?

CHAPTER IV

NOACHIDE AND MOSAIC LAWS

Whoever is righteous has regard for the life of his beast, but the mercy of the wicked is cruel.
Proverbs 12:10

Antithetical parallelism is common in early Hebraic poetry. Two contrasting ideas are brought together to make the same point. Like all the best proverbs it's short, sweet, and easy to remember. Proverbs 12:10 uses this device in a pretty self-explanatory manner: a person who is godly in all their dealings will extend their kindness to animals. A person who is cruel will treat them poorly, even if they think they're being kind.

Tragically, this can be seen in daily life. One only needs to look at the dogs, cats, and other pets who die in shelters; on average six dogs and cats per minute. [1] Or drive down a rural or urban street and look at the dogs tied to stakes or forced to live outside like sentient lawn ornaments. Drive to the suburbs and see dogs stuck alone in crates for 12-16 hours a day while their family ignores them. These people probably think that they are being kind; after all, they took the animal in, they feed and care for them, they may even give them vaccines or flea treatment as needed. However, by taking in an animal, you are making a contract with them to care for all their needs: mental, physical and emotional. By neglecting to care for the mental and emotional needs, they're not showing care for the whole animal, thereby breaking the contract. The righteous care for all the needs of their pets.

Why did King Solomon write this verse? In the first chapter, 2nd verse, Solomon explains that he writes the proverbs *for attaining wisdom and discipline; for understanding words of insight; for acquiring a disciplined and prudent life, doing what is right and just and fair; for giving prudence to the simple, knowledge and discretion to the young.* Solomon, regarded as one of the wisest men of the age, wanted to share his wisdom. He didn't just pull this idea out of the air. He was drawing on previous law and commentary with which the Israelites of the time were familiar. Humane treatment of animals was a minor theme throughout the Hebrew Bible and Christian Old Testament.

****

There are two types of laws in the Bible: Noachide laws and Mosaic laws. Noachide laws are the seven laws of Noah given by God for all of humanity. Adam had no laws, and the Earth descended into violent anarchy and chaos. After the flood, God handed Noah seven laws meant for all mankind to follow: do not deny God, do not blaspheme God, do not murder, do not engage in illicit sexual relations, do not steal, do not eat from a live animal, and finally, establish a legal system to ensure obedience to the aforementioned laws. Mosaic laws, on the other hand, are laws that God gave to Moses that are specifically for the Jews. These laws, including the Ten Commandments, are in the first five books of the Old Testament. Those five books are known as the Jewish written laws, or Torah. They make up a total of 613 mitzvot (commandments) that Jews strive to follow.

Animals, like humans, were created by God, a fact that God himself reminds Job of in chapter 40. Therefore, they are to be treated well. Adam was given the job of caretaker, a role that people are supposed to fulfill to this day. God included animals in the Noachide covenant in Genesis 9, and He included them in the Ten Commandments. The fourth commandment found in Exodus 2:8-11: *Remember the Sabbath day by keeping it holy. Six days you shall labor and do all your work, but the seventh day is a Sabbath to the Lord your God. On it you shall not do any work, neither you, nor your son or daughter, nor your manservant or maidservant,* **nor your animals,** *nor the alien within your gates. For in six days the Lord made the heavens and the Earth, the sea, and all that is in them, but he rested on the seventh day. Therefore the Lord blessed the Sabbath and made it holy.*

Genesis 2:2-3 states that on the seventh day God rested from all the work of creating the entire universe and designated the day as holy. It's no coincidence that laws regarding animals are found in both the Noachide and Mosaic laws. God intended for all mankind, not just the Jews, to show concern for the welfare of His creation. The fourth commandment (third for Catholics who have a different numbering system) tells us the importance of the Sabbath; it is a sacred day, important enough for God to mention it both in the second chapter of Genesis and in the Ten Commandments. This prohibition on work extends to all living things; Jews and Gentiles, servants, employees, and yes, even animals. Judaism and Christianity are unique in that no other religions require a day of rest for all people, let alone animals. Not only is all of God's creation supposed to rest, but we are also to keep it holy. God expected all of creation to respect this command.

Once again, we see allusions to the spiritual side of animal life. The command doesn't say 'let animals rest and humans worship;' animals are included in the entire commandment. However, as with all commands, it wasn't absolute; care and compassion still took precedence over laws. In Matthew 12, Jesus commanded us to still do good on the Sabbath, giving an example of a sheep falling down a pit. When someone sees an animal or person in need they still need to help them. God is reiterating humanity's role as caretaker. We are, in fact, our brother's keeper, responsible for the welfare for all life.

Exodus 23:10-12 emphasizes the importance of rest. *For six years you are to sow your fields and harvest the crops, but during the seventh year let the land lie unplowed and unused. Then the poor among your people may get food from it, and the wild animals may eat what they leave. Do the same with your vineyard and olive grove. Six days do your work and on the seventh day do not work, so that your ox and your donkey may rest and the slave born in your household, and the alien as well may be refreshed.* Once again, God is including animal rights alongside basic human rights. The poor, the homeless, and the wild animals were meant to eat from the fields that lay fallow every seventh year. God's concern for all His creation is evident throughout the scriptures.

Some of the same rights that God gave to humans, he intended for the animals as well. They are to rest on the Sabbath, and both humans and animals are allowed to eat from the produce they harvest. Jews are not allowed to muzzle an ox while he is treading grain (Deuteronomy 25:4). 1 Timothy 5:18, in the Christian New Testament, repeats this point. Timothy quotes that law, along with "a worker deserves his wages," yet again placing human and animal rights together.

The fourth commandment is a law that God expects humans and animals alike to obey, but by no means is it the only law instructing how people are to care for animals. Unnecessary cruelty is absolutely forbidden in Judaism. In the Jewish Bible and Christian Old Testament, it is taken for granted that animals have the same emotions and capacity for pain as humans. Jews recognize that animals are special because they were created by God. They understand that differences between humans and animals are a difference in degree, not kind, a concept later made famous by Charles Darwin. Laws regarding the emotional needs of animals can be found throughout the Torah. Deuteronomy 22:6-7 encourages compassion for the maternal feelings of mother birds: *If along the road, you come upon a bird's nest beside the road, either in a tree or on the ground, and the mother is sitting on the young or on the eggs, do not take the mother with the young. You may take the young, but be sure to let the mother [fly away], so that it may go well with you and you may have a long life.*

This passage recognizes the maternal feelings of the mother bird. Seeing her children taken from her would cause her much distress. By waiting until the mother flies off, she is spared witnessing the abduction of her young. Rabbi Moses Maimonides (Rambam) in his *The Guide for the Perplexed* [2] wrote:

In most cases, however, this commandment will cause the man to leave the whole nest untouched, because the young or the eggs, which he is allowed to take, are, as a rule, unfit for food. If the Law provides that such grief are not to be caused to cattle or to birds, how much more careful must we be that we should not cause grief to our fellow man.

Deuteronomy 22:6-7 ends with a promise of well-being and longevity: *so that it may go well with you and you may have a long life.* This is very similar to the fifth commandment (fourth for Catholics) found in Exodus 20:12 which instructs everyone to *Honor your father and mother, so that you may live long in the land the Lord your God is giving you.* It is not a coincidence that both laws involving parental relationships end with a promise of a long and happy life. The bond between mother and child is strong and it is important that one take great pains not to sever it.

Leviticus 22:27 and 28 instructs us not to separate an infant animal from its mother, nor are we permitted to slaughter a young animal with its parent on the same day. This is to prevent the young from being slain in front of his mother. Witnessing such an act would cause the mother much emotional anguish. Rambam, in his *Guide* wrote: *There is no difference in this case between the pain of man and the pain of other living beings, since the love and tenderness of the mother for her young ones is not produced by reasoning, but by imagination, and this faculty exists, not only in man, but in most living beings.*

Kosher dietary laws prohibit cooking an animal with dairy so that no young is cooked in his mother's milk. There is no major health benefit to this prohibition; it is directly related to the humane treatment of animals and the care and respect that one is supposed to show mothers of all species. It is disrespectful to the mother that her baby is killed and cooked in the milk she provides. It is not enough that the righteous regard the physical needs of their animals, they must also account for their mental and emotional well-being. The Talmud tells of Rabbi Judah ha-Nasi (135-220 CE), teacher during the occupation of the Roman Empire. Judah was a great leader whose influence with Rome [3] helped the Jews gain a reprieve from Roman oppression. However, he is most famous for compiling the Mishnah, the 63 treatises on rabbinical commentary of Jewish law. Babylonian Talmud Baba Metzia 85a tells the story of the suffering that Rabbi Judah endured, and the reason behind it:

Judah was outside one day, tending his garden, when a terrified calf ran towards the stern rabbi and hid in his robes. Judah realized that the poor calf had run from his owner who was taking him to slaughter. "Go!" Said the rabbi, "This is why you were created." The unfortunate calf left Rabbi Judah and was killed that day.

The story doesn't end with that tragic epilogue. No sooner had the calf left the rabbi's sight Judah developed a terrible toothache, followed by kidney stones, followed by a headache, followed by gastrointestinal distress. For years the rabbi suffered in this way. He prayed for peace, but the angels in heaven said "Since he had no pity on the calf, let us take no pity on him." On the thirteenth year of his ailments, his maid informed him that she found a nest of weasels. "Shall I swat them with my broom?" She asked, the good rabbi pondered this. "No." said he "Leave them be. For it is written: "[God's] tender mercies are over all His works." (Psalms 145:9)

The angels in heaven took note of the good rabbi's sympathy and proclaimed, "Since he is compassionate, let us be compassionate to him." Instantly Rabbi Judah was cured of all his pain. His toothache, kidney stones, headache, and stomach troubles all disappeared. Once more, for the first time in thirteen years, Judah could go about his daily life.

****

We are to show compassion to all God's creatures, as He shows compassion to us. There are many laws found in the Torah, and not found in other top five religious texts, concerning the physical welfare of animals. The first few verses in Deuteronomy 22 instruct us to return a lost ox or donkey to a brother if we happen to find him first. If we happen to find that their missing ox or donkey has fallen, we are to help the animal to his feet and then return him. This doesn't seem like a big deal; I would hope that most people who see a friend's or neighbor's lost pet would return him, especially if that pet was injured and needed help.

Exodus 23, however, takes it a step further. Verse 4 instructs those who see an enemy's ox or donkey wandering off, must still return the animal, and if they see that the donkey of someone who hates them has fallen under his load, they are instructed to help him with it. This shows concern for the animals, but by practicing this it will also lift the people onto a greater spiritual plane. (This is not dissimilar to Jesus instructing His followers to walk two miles for the despised Roman rulers in Matthew 5.) You may have a good reason for disliking someone but his or her animal is innocent; why should an animal in distress suffer because of your personal feud?

In Judaic/Christian/Islamic traditions, animals were created by God; therefore cruelty to them is absolutely prohibited. Jewish laws regarding animals are made to prevent *tza'ar ba'alei chayyim*: suffering of living creatures. Some of the biggest Biblical heroes were shepherds, (Jacob, Abraham, Moses, King David, and Amos) men whose livelihoods were based on caring for animals. Rebecca was judged to be a good person because she showed concern for the welfare of animals, offering to draw water for a stranger's camel. Conversely, Nimrod and Esau were hunters and were viewed as villains. To this day hunting, particularly sport hunting, is frowned upon by Muslims and Jews.

When animals are used for human benefit, we are instructed to take extra care for their comfort and safety. King Solomon in Proverbs 27:23 instructed his sons to know the condition of their flocks and to pay careful attention to their herds. By doing so both his sons and their animals would reap the benefit. Animals also benefit from God's blessings when Jews keep the Mosaic laws. Deuteronomy 11:13-15 says that if the Israelites keep the commands to love the Lord, he will rain down blessings. He will provide grass in the field for the cattle, and that there will be grain, new wine, and oil, and they will eat and be satisfied. Animals are included in our curses as seen in the last chapter, (page 76) but they are included in our blessings as well.

Where God provided laws for livestock, He similarly laid down laws for pets. In fact, Jews are to make sure that they are capable of caring for an animal before they even get one. They are required to feed all animals before they feed themselves. Adult humans, outside of a few unfortunate situations, typically know that no matter how hungry they are, they're going to get a chance to eat again soon. Wild animals and pets never know when their next meal is going to be; this can cause them mental distress. To prevent this unnecessary suffering, Jews are instructed to feed their animals first. Provided that meat and dairy are not mixed, pets can eat foods that are considered treif (non-kosher). However, for Jews that feel the need to have their pets follow a kosher diet, there is, at the time of this writing, at least one brand of dog food that is certified kosher.

Pets cannot be altered unnecessarily as it causes suffering. Therefore, declawing cats, and cropping the ears or docking the tails of dogs, is prohibited as there is no genuine need for the procedures and it causes them physical pain and distress. (Tail docking, for example, is performed on puppies less than ten days old, and is done without anesthesia.) Castrating any animal is prohibited under Jewish law, as it is believed to also cause unnecessary suffering; however, Jews are allowed to have an animal who has already been altered. Since modern pet practices consider the spay and neuter surgeries to be a necessary part of pet guardianship, observant Jews are strongly encouraged to get their pets from rescues where the procedure has already been carried out.

****

Since Christianity is a religion that branched off from Judaism, some of the same laws concerning the welfare of animals apply to Christians as well as Jews. In Matthew 25, Jesus taught that what you do to the least of [these brothers] you do to him, and when you withhold acts of kindness to the least, you withhold it from him. Many Christians apply those verses to animals and humans alike. Jesus was a rabbi, and when he differed from traditional Hebraic theology, it was noteworthy enough to make it into the Gospels (The books of Matthew, Mark, Luke, and John). It is not the words Jesus said in regards to animal welfare that show us how to treat them, it's the words he *didn't* say. He never contradicted laws concerning the rights and welfare of animals, therefore, we have no choice but to conclude that the Mosaic laws still applied.

On the famous Sermon on the Mount, Jesus spoke of the Mosaic laws, clarifying that the true intent behind the laws was to instill justice, mercy, and loving kindness in the hearts of the Jews. A change of hearts, not legalism, was the purpose of the 613 mitzvot that make up the Law of Moses. In Matthew 5:17-18, Jesus says *Do not think that I have come to abolish the Law or the Prophets; I have not come to abolish them, but to fulfill them. I tell you the truth, until Heaven and Earth disappear, not the smallest letter, not the least stroke of a pen, will by any means disappear from the Law until everything is accomplished.* He follows that by saying "you have heard it taught this.....but I tell you this..." clarifying many interpretations of the law with an even stricter version that focuses more on the listener's spiritual welfare rather than legalistic guidelines. Jesus' focus was on getting his listeners' hearts right with God and other people.

In Matthew 22, a Pharisee, a teacher of Jewish law, asked Jesus which was the greatest commandment. In verses 37-39, Jesus explains that Christians are to *Love the Lord your God with all your heart and all your soul and all your mind. This is the greatest commandment. And the second is like it: love your neighbor as yourself. All the Law and the prophets hang on these two commandments.* Many Christians are familiar with the Golden Rule; Jesus taught them to "do unto others as you would have them to do unto you."

In Jewish tradition, Rabbi Hillel, (110 BC -10 AD) was approached by a gentile who said "Convert me to Judaism on the condition that you can teach me the entire Torah while I stand on one foot." By saying that it must be done while standing on one foot, he was basically asking for a one or two sentence summary of all 613 mitzvot. A seemingly impossible request. Hillel, up for the task, said to him "that which is hateful unto you, do not do to your neighbor. This is the whole of the Torah, all the rest is commentary. Go now and study." In this story, Hillel, like Jesus, summed up the entire law in a nutshell, and they both said basically the same thing. What is important is how you treat others; what is important is love. All the laws of the Torah, all the laws of God, center around love; for God, for one another, and even for the animals.

The Jews and Christians were not the only sons of Abraham to follow a version of the Golden Rule. In the 13th Hadith, Muslims are taught that *None of you truly believes until he loves for his brother that which he loves for himself.* Of course, it's not just the Abrahamic traditions that follow the Golden Rule; the Eastern religions have their own versions of this rule. In Jainism, the Acaranga Sutra 5.101-2 teaches: *one who you think should be hit is none else but you, one who you think should be tortured is none else but you. One who you think should be enslaved is none else but you. One who you think should be killed is none else but you. A sage is ingenuous and leads his life after comprehending the parity of the killed and the killer. Therefore neither does he cause violence to others nor does he make others do so.* The Mahabharata 5.1517 instructs Hindus that *This is the sum of duty: do not do to others what would cause pain if done to you.* And finally, in Buddhism, the Udana-Varga 5.18 reads *treat not others in ways that you yourself would find hurtful.*

All the major religions teach that respect for others is the epicenter of their belief system. Should humans be so anthropocentric that they think their respect only begins and ends with other human beings? Jesus was a rabbi who shared the beliefs of traditional Jews. If Jesus, sharing the beliefs of traditional Jews, had intended that the laws concerning animal welfare no longer applied, it would have been significant enough to include in the Gospels along with all his other deviations from Mosaic Law. Christians are told emphatically to love and be charitable to those weaker than they: the elderly, the infirm, children, the impoverished, and yes, even animals are included under that umbrella. Without love, the law of the prophets is meaningless. In his first letter to the Corinthians, chapter 13:8 and 13, Paul writes that *without love he is nothing. Love never fails; where prophecies cease and knowledge passes away, love endures forever. Faith, hope, and love are three great virtues, but the most important of all of those is love.*

The Noachide laws were meant for all humanity to follow. Therefore, it is not surprising that God placed it in the hearts and minds of the religious founders from all traditions. Jewish philosopher Rabbi Moses ben Maimon (known as Maimonides or Rambam) believed that any gentile who observed the Noachide laws would have a place in the world to come. He wrote in the *Laws of Kings and Wars* chapters 8 and 9, that before Abraham, all commandments were universal. After Abraham, any non-Jew who kept the laws because they were commanded by the Holy One was regarded as of the Righteous of Nations. Anyone who observes the laws and doesn't believe them to have come from the Holy One, does not belong to the Righteous of Nations, but should nevertheless be held among the wise. Should it be surprising, then, that we see similar laws laid out among the righteous sages of the largest traditions?

****

Islam, like Christianity, is another religion with elements of Judaism. It also emphasizes love for all life and the humane treatment of animals, with some of the laws being the same. Animals, like humans, coming from the same creator, have some of the same rights. In the Abrahamic faiths, animals are believed to lack free will. Because of this view, Muslims consider animals to be fellow Muslims. They submit to the will of Allah by following their instincts and living to the laws of the natural world. Islam recognizes the emotional lives of animals so care must be taken to ensure emotional well-being. Laws similar to Mosaic laws, include the prohibitions against taking nestling birds away from their mothers. Tail docking and ear cropping are forbidden; one cannot take a pet unless they have the means to provide care; and of course, as previously discussed, there are many similarities between halal and kosher guidelines.

Because Allah loves animals, Muslims are also instructed to love them and to treat them with compassion. We must take care that we do not overload pack animals or overwork any animal. Neglect is forbidden. The Prophet Mohammed told the story of a woman who was sent to Hell because she locked up her cat. She did not feed the cat and prevented him from obtaining food for himself. Because of this neglect she was forbidden to enter paradise. There are prohibitions against sport hunting, fighting animals for sport, and factory farming. Animals can be used for and by people, but only if they are treated kindly. In Islam, one good deed is worth ten bad deeds. How one treats animals can determine whether or not one enters paradise. It is better to play it safe and to treat them kindly.

Animals have their own position in creation and we are responsible for their welfare. The Earth was made by Allah, and for his pleasure, therefore every living thing has its place, its purpose, and should be cherished. Quran 55:10 reads *It is He (Allah) who has spread out the Earth for His creatures.* Allah loves animals as He loves humans, and the Quran, along with the Hebrew and Christian Bibles, speaks of the spirituality animals' exhibit and the praise that they give to Allah. Quran 24:41-42 states *Seest thou not that it is Allah whose praises all beings in the heavens and on Earth do celebrate, and the birds of the air with wings outspread? Each one knows its own mode of prayer and praise. And Allah knows well all that do, yea to Allah belongs the dominion of the heavens and the Earth; and to Allah is the final goal of all.* Even the animals acknowledge their creator, as their creator acknowledges them. Quran 6:38 *There is not an animal that lives on Earth, nor a being that flies on its wings, but forms a part of communities like you. Nothing have we omitted from the Book, and they all shall be gathered to their Lord in the end.* This verse takes for granted that animals will take their place alongside humans in paradise.

All the Abrahamic faiths recognize that God, the creator of all life, loves his creation. This differs from religions that have no creator god, or those who view the creator as cold and indifferent. Islam regards cruelty to animals as a sin, and no different than cruelty against another person as both are sentient beings. Because animals cannot speak for themselves, it is up to us to take care of them. This is consistent with the Judaic teachings in Eden that placed humans as guardians over creation.

Because Allah cares for the animals, we are also instructed to care for them. There is a famous story of a sinner who saw a dog circling a well. Reasoning that because he was thirsty, the dog must also be thirsty, he used his shoe as a container and brought water to the dog. That act of compassion tipped the scales in his favor and upon his death he went to paradise instead of hell. The story takes on extra significance when one takes into account the status of dogs as "unclean." Allah wants us to extend our arm of compassion to all animals, clean or otherwise. This belief is held by all children of the God of Abraham. Jews, Christians, and Muslims are instructed to care for the animals, not for the sake of the human or animal, but because God himself cares for the animals.

****

Likewise, Sikhs also believe that God is the primary connection between all creation. They believe that there is a divine spark in the soul of all animals and all humans. Animals must be treated with care and respect; but because humans fail to have compassion, the world is being destroyed. Sadly, one does not have to look too far to see proof of this. Deforestation and extinction are evidence of how far we have fallen from our task.

Guru Nanak, one of the first Sikh Gurus, taught that the highest religion was to attain universal brotherhood, and to consider all creatures as equals. However, Sikhs believe in reincarnation and believe that while all animals have a soul, humans are the highest order of creation and the only ones capable of merging back with God. For those who have not purified their soul, they will get one more chance as humans before being sent back to wander the Earth as animals. However, treating all life with compassion is evidence of a purified soul.

****

The eastern traditions also value the lives of animals and have rules in place for their welfare. Buddhists strive to follow the Noble Eight Fold Path: 1) Right View- the wisdom to know the truth. 2) Right Intention or thought - the wisdom to free your mind from evil and eliminate the three poisons of greed, anger, and ignorance. 3) Right Speech -to speak the words of truth, words of compassion, words of praise, and words of altruism. 4) Right Action - working for the good of others and following the ten Wholesome Actions. 5) Right livelihood- to have a moral profession that has respect for life. 6) Right Effort- which is to resist evil. We are called to prevent unwholesome states of being, end unwholesome states that we already have, develop wholesome states that we do not have, and strengthen any wholesome states that we currently have.

7) Right Mindfulness- which is meditation and the desire to control one's thoughts. We can do that by being mindful of the body, our feelings, the impermanence of mind, and our mental qualities. 8) Right Concentration- which is meditation, to focus the mind and settle the body.

The ten wholesome actions of Buddhism are; do not kill any living being, do not steal, abstain from sexual misconduct, be honest, do not be prejudiced, avoid malicious speech, do not engage in gossip, do not covet, do not wish harm on others, and be open-minded. Complementing the ten wholesome actions are the ten unwholesome actions; the killing of any living being, stealing, sexual misconduct, false speech, slanderous speech, and harsh speech, gossiping, covetousness, wishing harm to others, and wrong views.

In order to follow both the Noble Eight Fold Path and the 10 wholesome actions, one must not harm animals. By following the path of right action, one must never harm an animal. And by following the path of right livelihood, one must never take employment with a company that harms anyone. Therefore, a Buddhist would be prohibited from working in a slaughterhouse or an animal testing facility. Buddhists believe that all actions acquire either good or bad karma. Mistreating an animal would bring bad karma, so Buddhists try to treat all life with respect.

The Dhammapada chapter X: 129-32 states *all tremble at force, of death are all afraid, likening others to oneself kill not nor cause to kill. All tremble at force, dear is life to all, likening others to oneself kill not nor cause to kill. Whoever harms with force those desiring happiness, as seeker after happiness one gains no future joy. Whoever doesn't harm with force, those desiring happiness, as seeker after happiness one gains future joy.* We should put ourselves in one another's place, have empathy towards all life, and not cause fear, harm, or death to any living thing. If we do it will bring bad karma. However, if we refrain from bringing fear and violence to others, we will obtain good karma.

As with the Abrahamic religions, animals are considered sentient beings, capable of physical and emotional pain. Buddhists believe that all beings, both human and animal, have a Buddha-nature; the seed of consciousness and cognition, and eventually this will lead to enlightenment. Humans and animals are closely related, and the key to civilization is the friendly spirit towards all life. Though a Buddhist must take care to treat animals kindly, they do believe that animals are spiritually inferior to humans. Bad karma will lead to rebirth as an animal, and since it is believed that animals are incapable of consciously acting towards self-improvement, the soul will remain in an animal until the bad karma has been worked off. Only humans have the spiritual ability to seek Nirvana.

****

Hindus, along with Buddhists and Jains, believe that animals have souls. Hindus believe that compassion and kindness should be the hallmark of treatment towards all life. When humanity violates these principles, everybody suffers because all life is interconnected. Animals, like humans, are subject to natural laws and to samsara, the cycle of life, death, and rebirth. Killing any living being stops a soul on its journey and is therefore recognized as a great evil.

Animals occupy a significant place in the Hindu religion, as gods will often take on animal form. Ganesha, the Lord who removes obstacles (and one of the most popular gods) is depicted with a human body and the head of an elephant. Vishnu, the second god in the Hindu triumvirate, can take the forms of fish, boar, and turtle. Humans are viewed as animals until they gain knowledge and shed their ignorance. Animals may carry a touch of the divine, but as in Buddhism, only humans are capable of attaining freedom from samsara, or moksha (spiritual perfection).

****

Kindness towards animals is considered a divine trait. Buddhists, Jains, and Hindus all strive to practice *Ahimsa*, or nonviolence to all living things. However, none show that devotion to compassion as well as the Jains. Jains believe they should strive to master the three jewels: right faith, right knowledge, and right conduct. To achieve those three jewels one must observe the five vows: *Ahimsa* (non-violence), *Satya* (truth), *Asteya* (non-stealing), *Brahmacharya* (celibacy), and *Aparigraha* (non-attachment). We can see the clear influence that Buddhism and Jainism had on each other. Of the five vows, *Ahimsa* is the most important, and the capstone of their religion. Jains believe in the equality of all living things, regardless of their size, ability, or spiritual capabilities. Not only does all life have a right to exist, every existence is necessary for there to be perfect harmony and peace.

Ahimsa is not just about physical non-violence; mental and emotional abuses are also prohibited. Jains recognize that sometimes harming life is unavoidable and unintentional. Nevertheless, practical, conscious steps must be taken to minimize harm. Furthermore, violence can go beyond the physical or mental act of violence. Conscientious Jains recognize that even the intent to cause suffering, any act that lacks compassion, and even ignorance itself could be encompassed in the circle of violence. Jains practice their religion through actions[3].

****

Each of the religions referenced in this chapter stresses compassion, love, and even respect for the natural world. Though different religious laws have been used to justify cruelty to humans and animals alike, they have also been at the forefront of social and animal welfare. The Abrahamic faiths recognize that God created animals and delights in their happiness. God himself takes pleasure in his creation; from the smallest millipede to the most spectacular Galaxy. Jesus said that God feeds the sparrows and causes the lilies to grow. We are to respect nature and love animals because they are valuable to God Himself.

Religions that have no creator still recognize that animals are valuable in their own right. All religions believe that kindness and mercy towards all life will help us along our spiritual journey, whatever that journey may be. However, only the God of Abraham delights in creation for creation's sake. By leading other faiths to the path of nonviolence, He provided greater protection to His creation. Loving kindness is

---

[3] Demographically, while Jains comprise less than 1% of India's population, they make up over half of the social welfare programs.

always rule number one. This Divine light can only come from one Source: the same which delights in the entire universe.

CHAPTER V

IMITATIO DEI

Look at the birds of the air; they do not sow or reap or store away in barns, and yet your Heavenly Father feeds them.
Matthew 6:26

In theology, lies the concept of *imitatio Dei*. Since man was made in God's image, we are obligated to imitate Him, not to be Him, but to try to live a godly life. Leviticus 19:2 tells us to "*Be holy, because I, the Lord your God, am holy.*" There's a popular Christian phrase "What would Jesus do?" We are called to be God-like in our actions. Christians strive to question what Jesus would do so that we may follow that same path and be aware of both our actions and their consequences. Luckily, there are guidelines on how to achieve this. The Hebrew and Christian Bibles and the Islamic Quran all speak about how pleasing creation is to the God of Abraham. God wants to share that joy with us; He wants us to delight in nature and wildlife as He does. To be cognizant and conscientious of it, to be aware of how our actions affect it. If God displays love and guardianship of the animals, then we are to be loving guardians as well.

There is the mistaken idea that the Bible is silent on animal welfare. This, of course, is far from true. One need not dig too deep in the book to see God's concern for all life on earth;

human, animal, and even plant life is enclosed in God's circle of compassion. Psalm 36:5-6 teaches: *Your love, O Lord, reaches to the heavens, your faithfulness to the skies. Your righteousness is like the mighty mountains, your justice is like the great deep. O Lord, you preserve both man and beast.*

Multiple Bible verses mention how God watches over the animals. He feeds the ravens, provides grass for the cattle, He watches the sea creatures swim, and the ostriches run, and it brings Him joy. The 36th psalm, which was written by King David in a moment of awe, sings of God's power and unfathomable might. David recognized that out of the millions of people who had inhabited the earth, all of the insects, reptiles, crustaceans, birds, and mammals, that God, creator of heaven and earth, takes a protective interest in all He created. David saw the love of God displayed throughout the skies and the entire world and it filled him with awestruck wonder.

Countless times, the Bible speaks of God's love for His creation. The book of Job tells the story of a righteous man who lost everything; his children, his home, and his fortune, over a wager between God and the devil. The story strives to answer the great theodicean question of why bad things happen. Naturally, Job complains about the unfairness of it all, and after a book's worth of elaborate speeches and poetry, God finally answers Job. He doesn't give him a reason for his pain. Instead, after 37 chapters of Job pleading, and his friends accusing him of being a terrible sinner, God responds.

Unfortunately for Job, it was not the answer he sought. God chastised him the way a parent scolds a child. He is the one who asks the questions, and even throws in a bit of sarcasm for good measure. (Chapter 38:21) Two chapters, 38 and 39, display His majesty, instead of a lesson on theodicy and human suffering, God gives a lesson on nature. In those two chapters God names a couple of the constellations, reminding Job that the entire universe is His. He speaks of the animals that bring Him pride and joy. He seems to particularly delight in the wildness of some of the animals; mountain goats, hawks, and lions, as they symbolize freedom and a lack of human control.

Ultimately, it's not humans who have dominion; rather it is God who is in charge. It was God, not man, who gave the horse his strength, it is God who counts the months until the doe gives birth to her young, and then keeps watch as the young fawn gains strength in the wild. By the wisdom of God, the hawk takes flight and the eagle soars at His command. God reminds poor Job of the power of the leviathan, a mighty animal beyond human might. God uses nature to illustrate His majesty, as He was creator of all, but also to humble Job. *Everything under heaven belongs to me* says God in chapter 41 verse 11. After all that, Job had nothing left to say save for this: *Surely I spoke of things I did not understand, things too wonderful for me to know.*

Some readers believe that Job was a historical person who lived about 200 years before Moses. Ezekiel 14:14 mentions Job by name, and they argue that this likely wouldn't be the case for a fictional character. Other people believe that the book was written as an allegory to explain how we aren't enlightened enough to comprehend suffering. They take issue with God literally placing bets with the devil at the expense of a human soul. They think that the larger picture is that we are incapable of understanding the glories and mysteries of God.

Irrespective of your philosophy on the book of Job, whether it is history or allegory, God was abundantly clear on how He views the universe. Man is not the apex of creation. Though we may hold a special place as we were made in His image, God takes pride in all His work. He loves the flora and the fauna; He eagerly awaits the birth of new animals and people. He knows the number of hairs on our heads, and dresses the fields in splendor. He revels in the beauty of the constellations and knows the exact dimensions of space. His love for His entire creation is beyond human understanding.

****

To learn more about God's love for His creation, we can return to the book of Psalms. These poems confirm what we learned from the book of Job. The psalms were poems and hymns written by numerous authors. King David was the biggest contributor, but many were written by other poets who are named at the beginning of each psalm, and about a third of them were written anonymously. Some of the poems cry out to God to help, others are philosophical, and others are songs of joy and worship. It is here that we find hymns of praise for God's love for all that is on and in the Earth.

Many psalms single out the individual care that God gives to each of his animals. Other psalms call for the animals to sing God's praise, Psalm 148:7 *Praise the Lord from the earth, you great sea creatures and all ocean depths...wild animals and all cattle, small creatures and flying birds, kings of the Earth and all nations, you princes and all rulers on earth, young men and maidens, old men and children.* The unnamed psalmist took for granted that all the Earth, regardless of sex, age, class, or even species, should praise God.

The Psalms is not the only book to speak of animals praising or worshiping God. The prophet Isaiah in chapter 43 verse 20 tells us that the wild animals honor God because He provides for them. In the book of Revelation in the Christian New Testament, 5:13, John of Patmos writes *Then I heard every creature of heaven and on Earth and under the Earth and on the sea, and all that is in them, singing: "To Him who sits on the throne and to the Lamb (Jesus) be praise and honor and glory and power, forever and ever!"* It is not just the angels and the humans who praise God, nor is it the higher order mammals, such as the great apes, elephants or dolphins. But every creature on the ground, and even those under the ground; moles, worms, rats, and lizards, and every creature in the sea; sharks, anglerfish, giant isopods, leafy sea dragons, and squids all fell down and sang worship to the God of heaven.

Returning to the book of Job, when his friends are criticizing Job, he responds in chapter 12:7-10 by saying *"But ask the animals, and they will teach you, or the birds of the air and they will tell you; or speak to the Earth and it will teach you, or let the fish of the sea inform you. Which of all these does not know that the hand of the Lord has done this? In His hand is the life of every creature and the breath of all mankind."* Job felt that his friends lacked compassion for his hardship; he did not believe that the animals would literally speak words to his friends. Rather, that his friends could learn by observation, for even the animals know who feeds them, even they know the hand of God is at work. Do they not revere God? Of course they do, for they can see His handiwork.

Though Job said this not to marvel in the spirituality and discernment of the animal kingdom, but instead, to shame his friends, we cannot escape that once again, the animals acknowledge that God cares for them. God himself confirms this in chapters 38 and 39.

****

While the Bible has many examples of the spiritual lives of animals, those who wish to can also look to science to find evidence of animal spirituality. In the pre-renaissance era and after the industrial revolution, it was fashionable for those in the scientific community to deny that animals were rational beings, with the capacity to feel pain and emotions (a trend that, for some, continues to this day). Though now, through brain scans, psychological testing, and field observations many scientists recognize that animals are capable of rational thought.

We know now that animal skin, like our own skin, is covered in touch sensitive nerve endings. We know that animals also have a thalamus, the part of the brain that, among other things, processes pain. And we understand through MRIs and the study of brain structures and neurochemicals that animals are emotional beings. However, long before the technology for brain scans existed, Charles Darwin researched the emotional lives of animals. He argued that emotions and mental abilities existed along a continuum. Through evolution, it was from the animals that humans gained the ability to experience emotions.

This presents a problem for some people who want a clear separation between animals and humans. It used to be thought that tool use was the thing that separates humans from animals; then they found that chimpanzees, corvids, elephants, and other animals have been manipulating tools for longer than humans have existed. (1) It was then believed that our ability to teach others was what separates humans from animals, until they found that animals have the capacity to teach. (2) In response to this, scientists redefined what it means to "teach;" lo and behold, animals still came through under the new definitions. Through scientific discovery, science has closed the gap between humans and other animals in regards to emotional thought, ability to feel pain, tool use, and teaching. In light of all of that, it is now argued that religion and spirituality are what separates us from our cousins in the wild. So along comes science to show us otherwise.

Jane Goodall, who dedicated over half a century to field observations of chimpanzees, has found that these wonderful creatures will dance (3) at waterfalls. The chimps, usually male, will shuffle from foot to foot, sway, stomp in the water, and may even throw rocks. After this display, which may last up to 15 minutes, the chimp will sit on a rock, his eyes never leaving the water. Sometimes they'll dance before a particularly heavy rain and violent winds. His actions are very deliberate and exhibit joyousness at life, and perhaps, even an awe of nature.

Goodall believes these dances may be a precursor to religious ritual. Is the idea so farfetched? Many ancient and tribal religious rituals involve dancing or combine dancing with weather. Water is not the only element that chimps have been observed dancing in relation to. Anthropologist Jill Pruetz, of Iowa State University, has observed a dominant male chimpanzee dancing before his group in front of a brush fire [4] in Senegal. While most animals panic at an approaching fire, the actions of the chimpanzee were deliberate. When necessary, the chimpanzees would appear to predict the movement of the fire and retreat, but they remained calm the entire time.

While Jane Goodall was the first to recognize that chimpanzees use stones as tools, more relevant to our discussion, chimps have also been observed using stones as ritual. They've been recorded hoarding specific rocks [5] to throw at specific trees. This behavior is deliberate, oft-repeated, and seemingly irrational. There is no benefit to be gained. It doesn't help them gather food or protect themselves. It is not part of play, and it comes at a sacrifice to them through the cost of wasted time and energy. Juveniles will place rocks in hollow tree trunks, an act viewed by some as reminiscent of the ritual cairns that have historically been found around human settlements. Humans have long used stones for shrines and burial markers; are we seeing the next step in primate evolution? Or has this behavior existed for thousands of years unnoticed by humans?

I find the latter explanation more plausible. We know only a fraction about our closest cousins, and at our current rates of deforestation and harvesting chimpanzees for bush meat, they will be extinct before we can learn more. What is interesting is that this ritual has only been observed in West African chimpanzees. The Indigenous peoples of West Africa have similar beliefs and will also leave stones at trees they hold sacred. Did one species learn the behavior from the other? Or are they both borne from the same instinct? Perhaps the continuum that Darwin spoke of applies to spirituality as well as mental and emotional capabilities.

****

Recent research into the neurosciences may hold the definitive answer to questions of animal spirituality. To learn more, we want to look at the brains of other animals. Specifically, we want to look at the limbic system. The limbic system gives us our emotions, but also controls such mental functions as learning and the formation of memories. Over the past several years researchers have investigated the spiritual experiences of humans. They have found that our spirituality, our sense of oneness, awe, and mystery, is found in the limbic (6) system. This system of the brain is shared with non-human animals, and is one of the more primitive areas of the brain. It may be possible that animals were having religious experiences long before humans set foot on the Earth.

The capacity for spirituality and religion serves no evolutionary purpose. Yet here we find it, stuck in the limbic system of not only our brains, but also the brains of other mammals and birds. Could it be that this was by design? Like an artist signing his name to a painting, did a Creator instill within us all a sense of the mysterious; of knowledge that there is a higher power?

The Bible answers that question. To the Book's original authors, it was taken for granted that, like humans, animals had a spiritual side. King David, the prophet Isaiah, and John of Patmos certainly wouldn't be surprised to learn of the spirituality of modern chimpanzees. Revelations 5 speaks of the animals singing praise; Isaiah 43 says the wild animals honor God; and Psalm 145 is one of many psalms that sings of animals praising God. The 9th and 10th verses say that because

God has compassion on all He has made, all He has made will praise Him.

The 104th psalm, briefly mentioned in chapter 3, runs the gamut of praise for God. It sings of His majesty and the purity of the Earth. Verses 11 and 12 sings of His care for the animals, how He provides water for all the beasts of the field, the wild donkeys, and the birds. Verse 14 implies God's vegetarian ideal, *He makes grass grow for the cattle, and plants for man to cultivate - bringing forth food for the Earth, wine that gladdens the hearts of man, oil to make his face shine, and bread to sustain his heart.* Verse 27 touches on the idea of animal spirituality and how they look to God for their daily provisions. Verses 17 and 18 speak of how God provides shelter for His animals. Verse 26 sings of the joy that God takes in His creation, that the animals were created "to frolic." God loves all of His animals for their own sake. This poem, whose author was lost to history, speaks personally, as if to God himself.

The Israelites were farmers and herders, practical people who lived off of the land. They had no romantic ideals about nature; to them it was wild and brutal. The author could be accused of not knowing his audience, but he was so awestruck by God's creation that he had to cry out, "to sing praise and rejoice" in the splendor that is the natural world. Everything on Earth works and comes together because a personal God wanted it that way. By God's own hand, animals are fed and protected. Psalm 36:6, written by King David, confirms that idea, saying that *"God preserves both man and beast,"* all species are encompassed in His tender care.

Finally, Psalm 50:10-11: *for every animal of the forest is mine, and the cattle on a thousand hills. I know every bird in the mountains, and the creatures of the field are mine.* God is speaking out against animal sacrifice. You can't buy His favor; it is absurd to even think that. He created the animals and He created people. What can we give Him that He needs? He neither eats the flesh of bulls, nor drinks the blood of goats. He'd rather His animals live and play than be killed before Him as an offering. A concept both Isaiah and Jesus confirm.

Isaiah 1:11-12: *"The multitude of your sacrifices what are they to me?" Says the Lord. "I have more than enough of burnt offerings, of Rams and the fat of fattened animals; I have no pleasure in the blood of bulls and lambs and goats. When you come to appear before me, who has asked this of you, this trampling of my courts?"* God desires mercy, not sacrifice as we learn from Hosea chapter 6:6 and 1 Samuel 15:22; in fact, 10 different verses in 8 different books all sing the same refrain. God doesn't want us killing His animals as atonement; He created them and takes pride in them. He wants us to not sin in the first place. He wants us to widen our circle of compassion. If we are to follow the moral concept of *imitatio Dei*, we must, like God, have mercy on all His works.

****

The New Testament of the Christian Bible doesn't speak much of animal welfare. Because of this, many Christians throughout history have taken a self-centered approach regarding animals: use them, abuse them, and consume them. This approach, of course, is as unchristian as it is immoral. The biggest thing that sets Christians apart from Muslims and Jews is their belief in a Triune God. Muslims and Jews believe that God is one being and feel the trinitarian concept to be blasphemous.

Christians believe that God, Jesus, and the Holy Spirit are three parts of the same God. If God delights in His creation, as the Old Testament makes abundantly clear, then Jesus delights in creation as well. He often referred to himself as the Good Shepherd, one who keeps vigil over his flocks, and who is ultimately willing to die for his sheep. He uses animals often in his parables, and in the book of Mark, chapter 1 verse 13, Jesus spent 40 days in the wilderness in the company of the animals, while the angels looked after him.

Of course, going out into the wildness among the animals was not so unusual for Jesus as he was used to animals. He was even born among them, in a barn, as they surrounded him in reverence. Aside from his parents, the first living beings to witness his birth were livestock; cattle, sheep, donkeys, and other humble beasts. Perhaps this is a parallel to the creation account told in Genesis: God created the animals first, then the humans. Mary placed the infant Messiah in a manger, a feeding trough, where he would be off the ground and kept warm and safe. It seems practical to do this, but how many mothers would feel safe placing a newborn in an animal's food bowl? The animals knew that Jesus was special. Perhaps this is another Biblical allusion to the spirituality that animals possess.

After Jesus' birth, it was shepherds whom the angels told of the Good News. Not kings, tax collectors, religious leaders, nor fisherman, but humble shepherds, those who assumed the role of guardians. This, of course, was not by accident but by design. The prophet Micah, some 700 years before the birth of the Christ, prophesied the coming Messiah, and in chapter 5 referred to him as a shepherd; one who with the strength of the Lord, will guard the flock and bring them peace.

Jesus had a humble birth and led a humble life. His purpose was to become the sacrificial lamb, thereby bringing salvation to all creation. Animals were cursed alongside humans after the fall. However, they were not forgotten. God remembered them in His covenants with Noah and Hosea, and they were blessed to be the first ones to witness the miracle of the birth of Christ. They are blessed enough and loved enough take part in our salvation.

The entire Old Testament builds up to the climactic birth and death of the coming Messiah. Though seldom mentioned, the spirit of Jesus is always there. He came to save us all from death and usher us into a New World. The prophets Isaiah and John of Patmos tell us that we will not be alone in that world; we will be in the company of our animal cousins. Salvation is for all.

Most Christians recognize this on a fundamental level, though it may be buried deep inside the more anthropocentric ones who claim otherwise and insist that heaven is only for humans. At Christmas no one makes a nativity scene devoid of livestock. Animals are presented alongside humans; some illustrations even depict them worshiping the Savior along with us. The nativity resonates within all Christians, and brings them a feeling of peace and well-being. It, as well as the story of Noah's ark, reminds us of our intended relationship with animals. For a fleeting moment every year, we are back in Eden, living in peace and harmony with all creation. And we are reminded that we will live that way once again in Heaven.

****

Returning to Mark 1:13, we learn *He was in the desert forty days, being tempted by Satan. He was with the wild animals, and angels attended him.* That one sentence in the Bible, one verse out of more than 31,000, tells us very little. It gives us almost no detail, but was significant enough that Mark felt the need to add it. Jesus had just been baptized by John and was at the beginning of his ministry. Mark tells us that the Holy Spirit sent Jesus into the wilderness for 40 days, away from other people, to overcome the active temptation of Satan.

Here, some scholars draw a parallel and contrast between Jesus and Adam. Adam, along with his helpmate Eve, was in paradise surrounded by tame animals. Jesus was in the wilderness surrounded by wild animals. Adam and Eve were tempted by Satan and failed, dragging humanity and all of creation down with them. Jesus was tempted by Satan and overcame, eventually bringing salvation to all creation.

****

The idea that a creator loves individual animals is unique to the Abrahamic religions. Whereas all religions teach compassion, the God of Abraham teaches us that we are to love creation as He loves it, because He loves it. This goes far beyond the mere concept of *imitatio Dei*, as there are clear guidelines spelled out in regards to animal welfare and animal rights. The 145th Psalm says that *the Lord is good to all; He has compassion on all He has made.* This is consistent with Genesis, God saw all that He had made and deemed it very good.

God appointed us servants of the Earth. Genesis 2:15 says that Adam was put in the Garden of Eden to tend to it and care for it, but it is not our land. Leviticus 25 tells us that it belongs to the Lord and we are mere aliens. God brought forth all the animals for Adam to name; He commissioned us as guardians over them. Because God cares for their well-being He entrusted their care to the only species that was made in His image.

Our special status as humans doesn't give us the right to exploit animals; that was never God's intent. We were given the privilege to tend to them, to love them as He does. As a reward, when we all reunite in Heaven, all species will be tame. The curse will be lifted and they will no longer fear us, and we will no longer fear them. As Isaiah 11 prophesied, the wolf will live with the lamb, and there will be neither harm nor destruction on God's holy mountain.

PART II

ANIMALS THROUGH THE AGES

CHAPTER VI

HISTORICAL TREATMENT OF ANIMALS

It should not be believed that all beings exist for the sake of the existence of man. On the contrary, all the other beings too have been intended for their own sakes and not for the sake of anything else.
Rabbi Moses ben Maimon

It is a tragic fact that mankind has a bad track record as guardians over the animals. Throughout history we have treated them with both compassion and abuse; kindness, and contempt. As previously discussed, God intended we live together in harmony. We share the world with animals, but our relationship with them has gone well beyond that. Encoded deep in our DNA, and buried in the corners of our brains, is our God-given role of caretaker. All animals, human and otherwise, have been known to display altruism and empathy. We may pride ourselves on art and music, but our guardianship is a significant factor in what separates man from beast.

As with all rules, there are exceptions. Koko, the well-known Western lowland gorilla at the San Francisco Zoo, has adopted kittens as pets. Tarra, an Asian elephant at the Elephant Sanctuary in Hohenwald, Tennessee, has formed an inseparable bond with a retriever mix named Bella. Ants have been found to farm aphids, dolphins have saved whales from becoming stranded, and countless online videos highlight examples of strong cross-species bonds among animal "odd couples." However, while both anecdotal evidence and documented cases exist of animals taking on a guardianship position, outside of this occasional bond or show of altruism, humans' place as primary caretaker is unique among all other animals.

****

Our bond with animals is well-documented and predates civilization. Archeologists have found a burial site in northern Jordan dating around 16,500 years ago of a human buried alongside a red fox. [1] What is interesting about this was that both the fox, who was believed to have been killed to be buried with his person, and the human were both moved at a later date. When they moved the man, perhaps so he could be buried with his mate, they moved the fox to be with them both. This suggests an awareness of an afterlife, and the belief that the human and fox would be reunited if they were kept together. This site predates domestication by many millennia and suggests that early man may have experimented with foxes as guard animals, companions, or hunting partners before eventually domesticating the grey wolf.

Our best bet at understanding the human/animal bond however, is to study the human/dog bond, as they were the first animals to undergo domestication. To get the clearest understanding of that process, anthropologists and archeologists look to ancient burial sites. Worldwide, dogs, more than any other animal, have had proper burials. Early man was not in the habit of burying random animal carcasses. Around prehistoric camps can be found the early dog prototypes who were buried intentionally, as well as animals who weren't buried that had been killed for food or scavenged.

There was also a notable difference in animal remains; animals used for food had many nicks and cuts in the bones, marks not found in animals kept as companions. Animals kept as pets, predominately canids were often found buried with their humans.

Remains found in the early Neolithic period (approximately 10,000 BCE-4,000 BCE) some 7,000 years ago suggest that the earliest humans recognized the individuality of dogs, and perceived them as being on the same spiritual plane as people. Some of these early dog prototypes were buried with trinkets, perhaps things that people thought the dog might enjoy in the afterlife.

The prevailing theory is that early human camps, made thousands of years before the first human settlements, likely attracted wolves. The more aggressive ones would have been killed off, while the tamer ones would have thrived on left over bones and animal remains. It is believed that the wolves may have been an extension of early tool use, as they could have provided safety while the earliest humans scavenged on carcasses. They also would have been of help while ancient man went on hunts for small prey. At camp the wolves would have sounded the alarm at potential threats. The ability to bark at the slightest provocation was purposely bred into dogs as humans sought out and encouraged that trait.

Alternate theories [2] based on the discovery of ancient jawbones of both species suggest that the domestication process began even earlier than previously thought. Early humans and canids may have been together before humans began eating meat. Some scholars believe that it was the human/wolf partnership that helped give humans the edge over our Neanderthal cousins, and led to evolution in our current form. In other words, it was dogs that made us human.

As humans and dogs continued to thrive together, genetic changes began to occur. [3] As our diets began to change from more plant-based to more meat- based, and in wolves from more meat-based to more plant-based, our bodies evolved to accommodate these changes. This caused changes in our cholesterol, metabolism, and digestion. In an effort to learn more about these early canids, Dr. Ya-Ping Zhang [4] of the Chinese Academy of Sciences has studied canine DNA. He has identified a specific gene, the SLC6A4, which carries serotonin to neurons. Serotonin is a neurotransmitter responsible for pleasant feelings among mammals, and may be why the earliest canids were less aggressive. SLC6A4 may be the gene that got passed along and helped with domestication. Interestingly, that same gene has also been passed along in the brains of humans.

Rather than being an isolated incident that happened by accident, evidence of this newly formed human/dog relationship has been found on all continents where early hominids dwelled; from all corners of Asia, to Africa, to North and South America. While science has been able to find out much about our early relationship with animals by studying ancient burial sites, they've also studied cave paintings. These paintings could theoretically have been used to communicate important information such as where the tastiest plants could be found, which toxic plants to avoid, or where the best water source was. Instead, they are mainly about animals. Any actor will tell you never to work with dogs and kids because they will steal the show; prehistoric artwork shows that this phenomena has been true from the beginning.

Not only do animals dominate the paintings, but they were often drawn in stunning detail. To date, we still don't understand the purpose of cave paintings; were they were religious or ceremonial? Or perhaps used as an ancient newspaper intended to transmit information? Some theorize that the paintings were related to hunting; however, both prey animals and predators have been drawn. The caves themselves were pretty remote and not easily entered. It remains a mystery why early man would go out of their way to trek inside the caves to paint. Prehistoric paintings have also been found on rock cliffs, though these are rarer as erosion has worn most of them away. We may never learn the artists' motivation, but if we could, it's possible that it would open up a whole new understanding of, among other things, how early man viewed animals.

Chauvet cave in France is one of the more intriguing sites of known cave paintings. It features several various sized rooms connected by passageways. 22,000 years ago rock fall sealed off the cave, perfectly preserving it until it's rediscovery in 1996. The paintings found in the cave date back some 32,000 years and depict horses, rhinoceroses, mammoths, bears, owls, lions, and about seven other species, both predatory and prey. Lions, mammoths, and rhinoceroses account for more than 50% of the artwork.

Archeological records tell us that those animals were not hunted at the time. This suggests that the artists weren't just painting daily life; they were able to catch the form and movement of the animals, suggesting a previously unknown skill and understanding of art. Did they simply have an aesthetic appreciation for those animals? Of course, we can't ask them.

Though the cave is a veritable treasure trove of stunning art, what's really fascinating is that found in the cave is a pair of footprints walking side by side at a normal pace. Even better, the prints belong to a small child and a wolf. Given the absence of a child's skeleton in the cave, the pace they appear to have been walking, and the location of the prints, we can safely assume that the wolf was not there to stalk and kill the child. Was the wolf guarding the child? Were they playing together while the parents painted? Were the paintings there hundreds of years before the child who was there exploring the artwork with his pet (a prevailing theory)? We may never know, but we can take heart that the bond that children and animals share is ancient and unbreakable.

****

It was only after humans had so skillfully domesticated dogs that they realized they could domesticate other animals and plants as well. This led to the development of farming and human settlements. After dogs came many animals, the most popular being goats and sheep, cats, cattle, pigs, and horses in order of domestication. This new relationship between domestic animals and humans proved very beneficial and allowed both species to thrive. The humans provided food, protection, and shelter for the animals in return for meat and fur or leather.

The domestication of goats dates back to around 10,000 years ago, based on evidence found in the Fertile Crescent. This occurred during the Neolithic Revolution, a time when humanity transitioned away from hunting and gathering and into the period of agriculture. Until the Industrial Revolution, mankind would not see an event so important and dramatic as the change that occurred during the Neolithic period. Goats very quickly spread across ancient Europe and eventually made their way onto every continent except Antarctica. Goats are very hardy and could be used for meat, milk, and hide, making them ideal for trade, travel, and farming.

Genetic studies of sheep show a similar history, suggesting that they both were likely kept in mixed herds together. Because sheep were so intensely bred for select traits, they are the only species of livestock that would not be able to survive on their own in the wild. The sheep's wild ancestors were not aggressive by nature, but were sociable animals with high reproduction rates; this made them ideal candidates for domestication. Animals were such an important part of the establishment of these early civilizations that their presence began to creep into the culture and belief systems as well.

Not long after the development of farming, early man began to tame cattle (from wild aurochs), sometime around 10,500 years ago. They were domesticated independently in the Middle East (taurine cattle) and in the Indian subcontinent (indicine cattle). [5] Both lines of cattle soon spread across Europe, Africa, and Asia, where the two lines bred both with each other and with local herds of wild aurochs. These cows provided meat (and eventually dairy), fertilizer, and leather for the early farmers. Because of their sheer size and power, the cows were also employed to pull carts and to work the land as draught animals.

The earliest evidence of domesticated cats was found in a grave shared with a human, dating to around 9,500 years ago in Cyprus. (6) What is interesting is that cats are not indigenous to Cyprus. This implies that early settlers intentionally introduced tame cats. Some scholars (7) theorize that the cat was actually domesticated 12,000 years ago. While there is, as yet, little evidence of that, it does place their domestication (8) during the Neolithic Period when early man began to first progress from hunter/gatherer to farmer. When early man was learning to farm and store grain, who better to protect the grain and seeds from pests? It is also worth noting that recent (9) findings suggest that prehistoric Egyptians re-domesticated cats in their current form. Buried cat and kitten skeletons suggest that Egyptian cats may predate the era of the Pharaohs (5550 BCE-30 BCE) by nearly 2,000 years.

Meanwhile, pigs began their domestication10 process in the Middle East, but were also domesticated in China and parts of Europe. In contrast to goats and sheep, who traveled and were traded throughout the world, pigs were domesticated independently from one another. They were first domesticated sometime between 5,000-9,000 years ago in more settled areas. Where sheep and goats were more ideal for nomadic communities, pigs did better on settled farmland. The pigs' meat was easily preserved, they reproduced quickly, and their omnivorism made domesticating them an easy process, and farming them became popular among the non-Jewish cultures of the world.

Horses were likely first domesticated in the steppes of Eastern Europe and Central Asia over 5,000 years ago. The steppes were brutal and cold. The fact that the horse was already used to such a climate made them well suited for winter climates in other regions. This made it much easier for the people in the Neolithic period and Bronze Age (around 3,000 BCE- 1,000 BCE) to keep and maintain herds. The earliest horses were used for meat, transportation, and warfare. Once people realized that horses could be ridden, it changed the course of civilization. People could maintain livestock more easily, keep larger herds on greater tracts of land, and travel greater distances. This likely made their world larger and opened up to them previously unknown opportunities.

During the domestication process, behavioral and physiological changes occurred. This is a permanent change; animals that have been domesticated can never revert to their former wild selves. In essence, they become a new creation. This domestication eventually led to civilizations and advancements in the success and growth of the human race. Humanity began to thrive when they accepted their role as guardians and worked with, rather than against, animals.

****

Once humans moved away from painting on caves, they still managed to capture the importance and symbolism of animals. Ancient Egyptian art depicts animals in a variety of ways; from household pets to avatars of the gods. Exotic pets; baboons, monkeys, falcons, and even gazelles, were sometimes found in ancient Egypt and care was taken to mummify them at their deaths. Although not as prolific as dogs and cats, they weren't uncommon, and as is often the case still today, they were often viewed as status symbols.

Cats are famously known as a revered pet of the Egyptians, but dogs were also quite common, especially for the upper class who could afford to take care of them. Cats were important members of a family and held in very high regard throughout the country. The export of cats was illegal, and the punishment for killing a cat was death, suggesting that cats were valued over people. Though more people in the upper classes could afford pets, for those who had them, regardless of socioeconomic status, and quite like today, pets were viewed as an extension of the family.

Any family who had a cat die, all the inhabitants of the house would shave their eyebrows as a sign of mourning, according to the ancient historian Herodotus, and any family who lost a dog would shave their entire body. Dogs were often carefully mummified upon their deaths and often buried in tombs with their people. Sometimes the dogs died first, other times they were killed when their people died. It was taken for granted that dogs and cats would accompany their humans to the afterlife, as the ancient Egyptians recognized both the individuality and the soul of animals.

Ancient Greeks and Romans held animals in very high regard and many gods had specific animals dedicated to them. Pets were common at the time, and dogs were the most popular, even though Greeks and Romans attempted to keep other, wilder animals as pets. Plato, Aesop, and Homer all speak favorably of dogs in their writings, and Plutarch wrote in *Life of Pericles,* that the loving affection we bestow on animals is part of our nature and a uniquely human trait. Plutarch felt that in many ways animals were superior to humans, noting that they possessed courage, enthusiasm, intelligence and strong moral principles. The Greek philosophers, coupled with the Judaeo/Christian religion, had a profound effect on how the Western world views and treats animals to this day. Pythagoras, believing that animals and humans have the same kind of soul, taught respect for all life forms.

Conversely, the philosopher Aristotle (384 BCE-322 BCE) believed that the more rational the being the more valuable they are. Therefore men, being more rational than women, were the superior beings, while animals, lacking any form of rationality are below humans. Not only do animals lack the capacity for rational thought, but their lack of language displayed intellectual inferiority as well. Accordingly, animals are for human use and have no right to life.

Aristotle was very speciesist and believed that humans were the center, not only of the entire world, but the whole universe. Aristotle believed that everything in nature and in the heavens was made for human use. This anthropocentric philosophy had an overwhelming impact on how animals would be treated and to this day shapes animal welfare practices in the west.

Despite Aristotelian sentiment, pets were believed to be valued family members. Dogs were often buried in tombs, many marked with epitaphs which celebrated the bond between the dog and his person. Farm dogs, hunting dogs, and shepherd dogs were all viewed as essential to the person's line of work, and guard dogs were seen as important to have around the house. It was recommended that people allow their dogs to sleep inside during the day, so that at night they would be well rested and able to guard. In the Christian Bible, Mark 7:28, a Greek woman remarks that even the dogs sit under the table and eat crumbs that children leave behind. The context of that statement was that Jesus' words should be for everybody, but that offhand remark does tell us that by the Greek and Roman era dogs had found their way inside the home.

Dogs weren't the only animals kept as pets in Ancient Rome and Greece. Monkeys, cats, birds, and even fish enjoyed their place inside the homes of their people. Based on ancient writings and artworks, pets may have been shown more affection and care by the Greeks and Romans than we provide for our pets today. Yet while pets were seen as beloved family members, that same courtesy wasn't extended to all animals.

Animals were hunted for food or sport, farmed, and even cruelly killed for spectacle. Elephants, lions, bears, and other animals were killed during the fun and games of the Colosseum while bloodthirsty onlookers cheered. Throughout its heyday, it is estimated that over a million animals were killed in combat either with each other or with unlucky humans, 500,000 of whom were killed in the Colosseum themselves. In both Greece and Rome animals also met their death as sacrifice to the many gods in painstakingly elaborate ceremonies.

Animals killed as sacrifice was very common throughout the entire Mesopotamian region. Most cultures were polytheistic and required animals to be ritualistically slaughtered in order to appease the gods. It was believed that sickness, pain, and misfortune were all caused by a vengeful god or gods and that the blood of an animal could end their wrath and reverses their fortunes. Such gruesome practices were common throughout the ancient world and still happen in some cultures today. The Sumerians would even use the intestines and organs of goats and sheep to divine the thoughts and intentions of the gods.

****

Traveling east, we can look at artwork from the Tang Dynasty (618-907 CE) to understand the relationship between the ancient Chinese people and their animals. Dogs were alternately kept as pets, workers, food sources, sacrifices, or honored as one of the twelve animals of the zodiac. With the exception of their role as sacrificial animal, dogs are still held in the same regard and for the same use today. It was believed that dogs were a gift from heaven. [11] Therefore their blood, considered sacred, and was often used to bind an oath of allegiance. During the Shang Dynasty (approximately 1766-1046 BCE), no palace would be completed without a dog sacrifice. Inside the palace, royal dogs were often treated quite well, and many stories are told about their life saving ability, heroism, and bravery.

Domestic cats in China date back to the time of Confucius (551 BCE-479 BCE), but recent archeological evidence shows they may have been in the area 5,300 years ago, towards the end of the Neolithic period. [12] These early cats may have been used both as hunters and as pets. For their role as mouser, it seems cats were treated quite well. With Confucius, came new attitudes about how to treat animals with respect. But unlike some cultures during the time period, animals were never revered or treated as gods.

The early Chinese began the practice of using silkworms for silk, which enabled them to reduce their dependency on animal skins as clothing. Parrots, pigeons, fish, tortoises, crickets, and grasshoppers were common pets throughout Chinese history. The Chinese also used cattle, pigs, goats, sheep, and yaks for food, transportation, entertainment, or farming. Horses were used for hunting and warfare, but were not ridden until around the 4th Century BCE. From prehistoric times, until today, the relationship has not seemed to change much between the Chinese people and animals; they are regarded as tools for humans to use or meat for them to eat, with the lucky few being kept as pets. This of course, is not unique to China, but can be seen in all cultures throughout the history of the world.

****

In ancient India, spurred partly by Hindu beliefs and practices, Indians honored and nurtured animals. They were used as vehicles for the gods and as avatars of the gods; they were used for divination, and often used as symbolism. Lord Dattatreya, for example, is always accompanied by four dogs who symbolize the four Vedas. Water buffaloes, goats, chickens, sheep, elephants, and cattle were all domesticated and used to work for the Indians in trades ranging from medicinal, recreational, commercial, military, food sources, farm work, commerce, sacrifice, hunting, fighting, and gambling. Dogs were used as pets, hunters, and guardians.

In Vedic literature we learn the story of King Dharmaraja who trekked up the Himalayas with his dog, his brothers and their families. The journey was long and arduous and one by one his brothers and their families died until it was only Dharmaraja and his dog left. At last, they finally made it to the top of the mountain where he was greeted by the god Indra, who praised him and offered him a ride to heaven in his chariot. As Dharmaraja began to board the ride, he called for his dog to join him. Indra forbade it saying that dogs were not allowed.

When King Dharmaraja heard this he refused to go along saying that he would not leave his faithful friend who depended on him. The good king told Indra that he would rather be on Earth with his dog than be in heaven without him, a sentiment that is shared by many. Upon hearing that Dharmaraja wouldn't leave his dog, Indra was touched and allowed them both to enter paradise. Once there, the dog was transformed into the Dharma, the god of proper living.

Because they were such a big part of everyday life, the ancient Indians had deep beliefs about animals and recorded much of it in the Upanishads. This makes it easy for modern researchers to understand the relationship between humans and animals 4,000 years later. It was believed that animals had the ability to communicate with the gods and so it is not unusual to find evidence in Hindu mythology of the animals attempting to gain knowledge from the sages. Despite the fact that Hindus recognize no spiritual difference between the animals and humans, animal sacrifice was common in ancient India, and is still practiced today in some of the more remote regions of the country.

****

In the Near East sheep and goats were domesticated and used for commercial purposes dating back several thousand years. For the early Hebrews they were the main source of meat and milk, but also used for wool, and sacrifice. Animal sacrifice was big business for Jerusalem, a landlocked city far from trade routes. The Hebrew Bible, the Christian New Testament, and writings from historian Flavius Josephus, all depict the city, and especially the temple, as an economic powerhouse fueled by the blood of the young animals who were sacrificed. This essentially created Christianity.

The final nail in Jesus' coffin was his encounter at the temple. Mark 11:15 -19 describes how Jesus, in opposition to the sacrifices, burst into the temple, overturned tables, and drove out the currency converters. It was only then that the teachers of the law and the priests began to plot his execution. Teaching radical theories is one thing, disrupting the economic underpinnings of a large metropolis was quite another. This led to his death and, Christians believe, his resurrection which created the entire Christian movement.

Of course, the Israelites were not alone in the ritual practice of animal sacrifice. It was common practice throughout the ancient world, and one of the many ways ancient man had disregarded his role as caretaker. For the Israelites, the practice was particularly egregious as it symbolized how far man had fallen. Judaism was unique at the time of its foundation as a religion that placed humans in the role of guardian. Judaism taught compassion before Hinduism evolved into a kinder religion, and before the development of Buddhism and Jainism.

Despite the condemnation of slaughter by the prophets Isaiah, Hosea, Amos, Micah, and Jeremiah, the Israelites not only engaged in the practice, but turned it into a big business. In spite of the warnings from these prophets; animal sacrifice had a substantial impact on the economy, and as such would not be given up lightly. Sadly, this practice continues, to this day governments and business leaders put industry before animals. Archeological digs have uncovered city dumps containing animal bones corroborating the historical documents and Biblical accounts of the mass ritual slaughter.

Animal sacrifice may have played a major role in the life and livelihood of the Israelites, but Israel was an agricultural society and many other domestic animals were an important part of everyday life. Domestic animals were of great value to the Israelites and cruelty against them was absolutely forbidden by Hebraic law. Donkeys and mules were used for transport as road conditions did not favor carts or carriages. Donkeys, along with cattle and oxen, were also used for plowing fields and threshing grain. Because of the difference in size between the ox and the donkey, Jewish law considered it *tza'ar ba'alei chayyim* (or cruelty to animals) to yoke them together while working. Otherwise one would be frustrated and the other would be overworked.

Mules were not allowed to be bred according to Levitical law (Leviticus 19:19) that forbade breeding different animals. However, they were hardworking animals in the region, and it was common for the Israelites to import them. The dominion over animals that God granted humans implied a responsibility towards their welfare. This, combined with the other Biblical commands laid out in the Jewish Bible, had a profound effect on cultural attitudes towards animals that trickled into Christianity and Islam.

There is no record that the ancient Hebrews kept animals as pets, though there is evidence that some may have regarded their farm animals as pets or valued family members. In the region of Jericho, several hundred years before the Israelites invaded, the remains of cats and dogs kept as pets have been found by archeologists. However, there is no evidence of them after the Israelites arrival. Dogs existed in the region, but were seen as scavengers and therefore were "unclean," a belief that is shared by Muslims.

Dogs are mentioned quite a bit in the Hebrew and Christian Bibles, but almost always in a negative context. To this day, some Orthodox Jews will not keep dogs as pets. There is not a single mention of cats in the Bible, despite the fact that they were common in the region. And in spite of the fact that they are quite skilled at pest control, there is no indication that they were kept as pets or put to use around farms.

The prohibition against *tza'ar ba'alei chayyim,* not only prevents suffering, but also commands positive care. 12th century Jewish sage

Moses Maimonides (also known by the acronym Rambam), first person to write the Jewish code of law, believed that animals had the souls of rational beings. Maimonides recognized the moral worth of animals, their relevance to God, and their own sentience. He taught that eating meat was prohibited for Jews because living things have a degree of spiritual superiority. In his *Guide for the Perplexed* he wrote: "*It should not be believed that all beings exist for the sake of the existence of man. On the contrary, all the other beings too have been intended for their own sakes and not for the sake of anything else.*" Maimonides had tremendous influence on Jewish, Arab, and Western ideology. It is said that from Moses (the prophet) to Moses (Maimonides) there is no one like Moses.

****

In the Arabian Desert, around 1,000 BCE, lived the Bedouins, who occupied the land until Islam was founded in 622 CE. The Bedouins were nomadic animal herders, who moved to the desert in the rainy season and back to more cultivated areas during the dry season. Their livelihood was largely dependent on animals in some form or another. They herded goats and sheep, and camels were used for trading and warfare when necessary. The Bedouins depended on animals and worked very closely with them. Both good and bad qualities found in humans were attributed to animals, and it was believed that after death, the soul takes on the form of an owl as it leaves the body. To this day there are still remote tribes of Bedouins who live much like they did thousands of years ago, though they have included modern technology into their lifestyles. Approximately 35,000 Bedouins occupy the Aqueba region of Southern Jordan, as of this writing.

****

In 610 CE, Mohammad (570 CE-632 CE) first reported hearing revelations from God, which eventually led to the creation of the religion of Islam. Life in the Arabian Desert was brutal and animals and humans alike often suffered from both the harsh environment and human cruelty. After Mohammad, came clear rules on how to treat both people and animals. Mohammad proposed to his followers that Allah loves and cares for animals and placed injunctions against treating them cruelly or gambling on animal fights.

Animal sacrifice was common and continues to be practiced in many predominantly Muslim regions throughout the world. The Quran, with elements of the Hebrew Scriptures, lay down clear guidelines on the ethical treatment of animals, their welfare, and rules that they are not to be killed except out of necessity. However, animals are not regarded by all Muslims as possessing souls. Some believe that animals may not make it into paradise, however, how one treats them can determine whether or not a human can enter heaven or go to hell after they die.

These beliefs have been consistent with the Muslim community from its creation in the 7th century to present day. Early Muslims, like the Bedouins before them, lived off the land and domestic animals were a necessary part of their life and livelihood, particularly sheep, goats, and camels. Cats were common pets throughout Arabia in the Middle Ages, most Muslims saw them not as pets, but as respected family members. Similarly, birds were also of importance; as symbolism of the soul, messengers, and protectors.

Mohammad apparently cared for animals, and is said to have had a camel that was like a pet to him. He was walking the streets one day and came across a young man sitting on a camel as one would sit on a chair. Mohammad rebuked the youth and told him to either ride or get off, but "do not turn your animals into a chair." Animals have a right to rest just as humans do.

Mohammad had a tabby cat named Muezza that he was quite fond of, reportedly preferring to be cold, rather than disturb his cat who would be sleeping peacefully on his cloak. A sentiment with which many cat people can relate. According to another legend, Mohammad was called to prayer one day and his cat was asleep on the sleeve of his robe. Choosing not to wake Muezza, he cut off the sleeve and attended prayer while the cat remained sleeping. Ever since that day, the tabby has the letter "M," the mark of Mohammad, on their foreheads.

****

The Early Christian Church began as a Jewish sect and so they viewed animals in the same way the Hebrews did. Animals were a natural part of life and care must be taken not to cause them intentional harm. They kept kosher dietary laws and followed the same customs as the Jews, with the exception of animal sacrifice. Christians believe that the crucifixion of Jesus the Christ was the ultimate sacrifice thereby rendering animal sacrifice obsolete. Some of the earliest Christians practiced ethical vegetarianism and extended their circle of compassion to all creation. By and large, animals were viewed as a useful and necessary part of life.

Aside from the death and resurrection of Jesus, arguably the biggest event to shape Christianity was the conversion of Saul of Tarsus (approximately 4 BCE-62 CE), later renamed Paul. Saul was a Pharisee who believed that Jesus violated Jewish law. He made it his mission to jail and kill any follower of Jesus, who were at the time known as the Nazarene Sect. While on his way to Damascus, sometime between the years 33-36 CE, a bright light appeared and blinded Saul and the voice of Jesus commanded him to stop persecuting the Christians. Immediately Saul became a new man with a new name and a new mission.

Nobody is more zealous than a convert, and the newly named Paul led an effort that spread Christianity far and wide. The original Disciples of Christ were Jews who spread the word of God to other Jews and retained the Jewishness of Jesus. Paul, on the other hand, abandoned his Jewish roots and focused his ministry on the Gentiles. This eventually led to a split between the Jews and Christians creating two separate religions. Christianity began to lose many of the customs of the Israelites, including kosher dietary laws. Paul himself appeared to have no love for animals, using their names as insults, and arguing that Mosaic laws concerning animal welfare were written for human benefit rather than animal rights. This had an impact on some Christians who, to this day, cite Pauline beliefs and opinions as an excuse to neglect their role as guardians over animals.

The early Christians retained the Jewish beliefs that humans had dominion over the animals. However some of the church fathers had differences in opinions over what that entailed. The laws and poems in the Old Testament systematically expound upon how our dominion implies stewardship and responsibility over animal welfare. However, many of the leaders of the early church believed that they had no worth beyond their usefulness to humans. By the 4th century, Augustine (354 CE-430 CE), like Aristotle before him and Aquinas after him, believed that animals lacked rationality. He believed that we were made in God's image by way of intellect. It was common belief at the time that the rational mind was linked to the soul. Augustine believed that humans were superior to animals and that Jesus only offered salvation to rational beings.

13th century theologian Thomas Aquinas (1225 CE-1274 CE) was greatly influenced by Aristotle's views on the rationality of animals, and he confirmed the philosophy of Augustine. Aquinas believed that animals were of no inherent value and only put here to be used by humans, a belief that is held by some members of the church to this day. On closer examination, this philosophy fails to hold water, many animals either cannot or will not be of any use to humans, and most are considered pests or nuisances. Modern humans have the advantage, through brain scans and other technology, to know that animals are conscious beings with their own value. During the 13th century, people had no such assurances.

We know through the Bible that animals are valuable to, and beloved by, God. Aquinas did not share the Biblical sentiment of The Psalms or the book of Job (as seen in chapter 5), and ignoring scripture to the contrary, he believed that only humans were capable of understanding or worshipping God. Humanity is worth more than animals because we were the ones made in God's image (*imago Dei*) and only humans have free will. Aquinas believed that we alone have language and consciousness.

Aquinas believed that there was a hierarchy of life; plant life, animal life, and human life, with some overlap in between. (13) The lowest order of animal life is on par with the highest order of plant life, and the lowest order of human nature was on the continuum with the highest order of animal life. While Aquinas didn't hold that animals had value in their own right, he did teach his followers to treat them kindly. He believed that cruelty to animals could infect the human soul, but kindness towards animals would allow people to grow to a greater spiritual plane. This belief proved invaluable to animals for generations to come as it helped to facilitate the animal rights movement in later centuries.

CHAPTER VII

THE MIDDLE AGES AND ANIMAL SENTIENCE

The time will come when men such as I will look upon the murder of animals as they now look on the murder of men.
-Dimitri Merejkowski, in his book The Romance of Leonardo Da Vinci

By the 17th Century, the Aristotelian theory of animal irrationality lived on and was expanded by famed mathematician and philosopher, Rene Descartes (1596 CE-1650 CE). Descartes, regarded as the father of modern philosophy, had an enormous, albeit negative, influence on animal welfare. People could easily observe many behaviors that indicated conscious thought processes in the actions of animals. Many philosophers would explain away those behaviors by claiming a sixth sense. Descartes, however, believed that animals were like machines, mere automatons acting on impulse with no ability to reason. Humans, being capable of speech and the expression of ideas, are the only beings with souls and intelligence.

Because animals were not regarded as conscious beings, there was no ethical reason to treat them with care or concern. The consciousness, believed by Descartes to be located in the pineal gland, was what gave humans a soul. For Descartes, the belief that animals lacked conscious thought meant that they also couldn't feel pain. Unfortunately for the animals this opened the door to vivisection. Descartes would cruelly experiment on live animals; nailing their paws to boards and cutting them open, laying his hand on their still beating hearts. Scalding them, mutilating them, and cutting the infants from their mother's wombs were actions that had no moral consequences in the mind of Descartes, as the painful cries they made were evidence, not of pain, but of a broken machine.

Many other medieval philosophers and theologians shared the opinion that animals were incapable of reason. In the modern era, we can still find scientists who cling tightly to this belief in spite of mountains of evidence to the contrary. Likewise, in the earlier centuries, the great thinkers of the day had to do quite a bit of mental gymnastics to conclude that animals were irrational. Cognitive dissonance, ironically, can lead humans to hold onto beliefs that are themselves quite irrational.

Observation told the layman that animals were quite capable of rational thought and the ability to make decisions. For the philosopher and the theologian, this flew in the face of what they perceived as the superiority of man and the uniqueness of the human soul. In response to this, philosophers would claim that animals possessed a sixth or even seventh sense to account for seemingly rational thought processes. A practice that is still seen today among scientists who reject the notion of animal consciousness.

Can scientists or the early philosophers claim that an animal has no feeling if the subject itself has never been scrutinized? Maintaining, without evidence, that an animal lacks sentience is prejudice. Worse still, it's an unscientific ideal, held fast in the name of science. Yet for a scientist to claim that animals have emotions leaves them open to accusations of anthropomorphism, a cardinal sin in the scientific community. Perhaps tellingly, many of these same scientists have cats and dogs with whom they bond quite closely. These scientists and animals connect on an emotional level, and, at least subconsciously, the scientists must recognize the shared emotions. Nevertheless, they publicly deny the capacity for any such feelings in the so-called 'lesser species.'

The theory that humans are superior to animals by way of our speech and rational minds falls apart under scrutiny. Many humans lack the ability to speak, and sign language is a relatively recent form of communication. Some cultures throughout the ages have believed that deaf-mutes were punished by a god or gods and refused to help them. Those unfortunate people, while they lacked the ability to communicate, were still rational beings with souls and intellect. Infants lack language as well, and communicate in some of the same ways that other animals communicate, but nobody has ever argued against the soul of an infant.

****

Conversely, we know that animals communicate quite a bit and some have a "language" that is not dissimilar to ours. Parrots can speak whatever language they are taught, and experiments with the African Grey parrot, "Alex," have shown us that they possess a deeper understanding of language than previously believed possible. Alex (1976-2007) is the only known non-human animal to ever ask an existential question; when he looked in a mirror and asked "what color?" This indicates a self-awareness that even higher order primates seem to lack. He was aware of who he saw and was curious about his own being.

As per his personality, he knew what he wanted and was not afraid to ask for it. If he was bored he would misbehave or ask to be taken home. If he saw jewelry he liked, he would ask to keep it. He would also ask to go on walks, or play, or to be stroked. He sometimes behaved more like a spoiled or demanding child, holding the researchers hostage with his emotional outbursts. Should he not get his way, he would throw a tantrum, much the same way a human toddler would. On the other hand, when he was so inclined, he would behave like an angelic child. This range of emotions can only come from a complex brain.

Alex's handler, Irene Pepperberg, believed his intelligence to be on level with five year old humans, while he had the emotional maturity of a two year old. Alex had a vocabulary of over 100 words. He wasn't merely mimicking what he heard, howbeit, as he had an understanding of what those words meant. He was able to use those words in a meaningful context. Tragically, Alex passed away on 6 September 2007, at the relatively young age of 31. The cause of death is believed to be either heart attack, fatal arrhythmia, or stroke. His last words to Pepperberg were "You be good. I love you. See you tomorrow." Those daily parting words likely took on greater significance to Pepperberg after his death.

Where Alex communicated verbally, Koko the gorilla communicates through sign. She is so knowledgeable that she has a greater grasp of American Sign Language than do most people. She was born at the San Francisco Zoo on July 4th in 1971 as Hanabi-Ko (Japanese for "fireworks child") and shortened simply to "Koko." She achieved fame as the subject of the longest running and most ambitious experiment to teach language to another species, and is living proof of the intelligence of other primates.

Koko knows over 1,000 signs and understands over 2,000 English words. Penny Patterson, her handler, believes her intelligence to be on par with a three year old human. She is able to communicate her desires, needs, and even her emotions. She has an understanding of death, signing that deceased go into a "comfortable hole," and has expressed grief and sorrow at the passing of her kitten "All Ball," her companion "Michael," and even comedian Robin Williams, whom she had previously met. In the past, Williams had provided comfort and laughter to her while she mourned Michael.

Koko is unique because she is in an enriched environment and she has the opportunity to learn more than the average ape. However, she is not the only primate to use signs and gestures to communicate. In zoos and in the wild, gorillas have been found to know over 100 different signs. Researchers from the Department of Psychology at the College of Staten Island have proposed that signs and gestures have played a role in the evolution of language. Bonobos, chimpanzees, and humans all begin to rely on gestures to communicate at around a year old. As humans begin to learn to speak, they use gestures and signs less frequently. Interestingly, research by F.G. Patterson in 1978 [1] and S. Savage-Rumbaugh in 1986 [2] has found that bonobos, gorillas, orangutans, and chimpanzees, can use a rudimentary form of language (when allowing for limitations on syntax and vocabulary) when reared in an enriched environment. This is important as it shows that language is not unique to humans.

Birds and primates are both known for their intelligence, so it shouldn't be too surprising that they can possess an understanding of language and symbols. They aren't alone in their intelligence; however, a border collie named "Chaser" has a vocabulary of 1,022 words and understands nouns, verbs, prepositions, and adverbs. Chaser was trained for three years, after which her people no longer had the time to continue her training. Had she continued to learn at the rate they were going, it is very likely that her vocabulary could have doubled or quadrupled as of the time of this writing.

Chaser understands that the names of objects are names, and not commands, and can categorize and label many objects. For example; she understands that "toy" can mean any number of the over a thousand things that she is allowed to play with. She understands the proper name of the toy. And finally she understands the generic name, such as "ball," her favorite being the little blue racquet balls. She has been independently and repeatedly tested under controlled conditions. By studying Chaser, researchers have found that dogs can have extensive vocabularies, and a deeper understanding of the meaning behind the words. This opens the door to further research into whether such capabilities can be found in other breeds.

The intelligence of Chaser may surprise some people who have dogs, but not most. The majority of dog guardians speak to their dogs in the same manner that they would speak to a small child. This behavior is reinforced when the dog pays attention to the person's facial cues, listen to the speech, and then responds accordingly. The average dog understands 50 words, this is a limitation on the person behind the leash, since we know that dogs can comprehend more. The average dog guardian understands the communicative ability of dogs to a greater degree than researchers simply because they live with them and interact with them daily.

What does all this mean? To what extent does language and communication prove worth? To the early philosophers, it meant the difference between having a soul or not, being special or only worth what you could provide. In strictest terms, it meant the difference between life and death. But is it an apples to apples comparison? Are we to argue that these animals; the birds, apes, and dogs, are worth more than a human with a more limited vocabulary, or should we conclude that all are special in their own right?

The argument that humans are superior over animals because of our rational mind also fails upon closer examination. It has recently been found that ravens possess the ability to plan. Researchers are now turning their attention to parrots to see if they are capable of the same. Previously, only dolphins and primates have been believed to have that trait. Until as recently as a decade ago, humans were thought to be the only species capable of this ability. Meanwhile, throughout history a minority of humans have suffered mental disorders that would place their IQ well below that of an ape or other higher order mammal. Yet few would argue that those humans were inferior to animals or that they lacked souls. Cognitively, an adult chimpanzee is smarter than a 9-month old human infant. Does that mean that the infant is of no value and has no soul?

Through rigorous testing, and modern technology we can better understand the intelligence and communicative abilities that other animals possess. Understanding the intelligence of other animals does not detract from the intelligence of humans. Early philosophers and theologians didn't have the advantage of brain scans and controlled testing. While some were eager to deny them intelligence, many others understood that animals were conscious beings, they understood this even without the advances in research we have today.

****

In contrast to Cartesian ideology, world renowned painter, inventor, sculptor, scientist, and all around genius, Leonardo da Vinci (1452 CE-1519 CE) could very well add animal welfare advocate to his resume. As a genius with an insatiable appetite for learning, da Vinci would often procure the corpses of animals and humans with the intent to dissect them in an effort to achieve greater understanding. An activity that was less than legal. His effort paid off, however, as it led to a more intimate knowledge of both species. He used his interest in science to improve his study of art which led to paintings and drawings with amazing detail of both human and animal anatomy.

Hundreds of years before Darwin, da Vinci's experimentation allowed him to see the similarities between humans and other primates. In his collection of writings, *Thoughts on Art and Life*, he wrote "The description of man, including that of such creatures belonging almost to the same species, such as apes, monkeys, and the like, of which there are many." He wrote extensively about the limbs of both humans and animals and compared the bipedal motion of man to the quadrupedal walk of animals. *"The way of walking in man is similar in all cases to the universal way of walking in four-footed animals, because, just as they move their feet crosswise, like a trotting horse, so man moves his four limbs crosswise. Write a Special treatise to describe the movements of four-footed animals, among which is man, who in his childhood also walks on four feet."*

In his notebooks he wrote that both humans and animals have the capacity to feel pain, and noticed that physiologically; from our stomachs, to our muscles, to our veins, we're not so different. Hundreds of years before Darwin shocked the world with his theories of evolution, da Vinci wrote that nature, a 'cruel stepmother,' desired only reproduction, not life. The only purpose of life, according to evolutionary theory, is to pass on our genes.

Perhaps because he studied animals in such great detail, he had a greater appreciation for them than his contemporaries. Legend has it that he would buy caged birds from the marketplace, bring them home and release them. To da Vinci, the idea of any animal suffering was repugnant. He abstained from meat and dairy, believing it to be immoral, and calling man a "tomb for other animals." At times, he could even be accused of misanthropy, claiming that man was not King of the Animals, but King of the Beasts.

Da Vinci at times felt that men were morally inferior to animals. Sometimes he even extended his passion to claim that man was intellectually inferior as well, stating in his notebook that *"Man discourseth greatly, and his discourse is for the greater part empty and false; the discourse of animals is small, but useful and true: slender certainty is better than portentous falsehood."* Da Vinci was one of the few people of this period who extended his mercy to animals, a position more unique given that most people who shared his views were monks and nuns.

****

St. Basil (330 CE-379 CE), 4th Century Archbishop of Caesarea, took seriously the belief that our dominion over the animals was a command for servitude. He felt that it was a sin that the dominion we exerted over animals was what he called "ruthless cruelty." Instead he felt that we should exercise fellowship and compassion to all living things. St. Basil was one of the first Christian-era theologians to argue that animals had worth in and of themselves.

In the 5th Century, St. John of Chrysostum (approximately 347 CE-407 CE) believed that since humans and animals come from the same origin, we should show kindness towards them, stating "Surely we ought to show kindness and gentleness to animals for many reasons, and chiefly because they are of the same source as ourselves." An echo of what God told Job in the book named the same. St. John taught that the human ability to feel compassion towards animals was proof that we are related. In the 16th century, another St. John (1542 CE-1591 CE), this one St. John of the Cross, taught that animals share with us the concept of *imago Dei* and that they, like humans, possess an immortal soul. Like many of the Biblical authors, he believed that the animals exalted God.

Perhaps the saint most famous for his kindness towards animals was St. Francis Assisi (approximately 1181 CE-1226 CE) in the 13th century. St. Francis taught that it is not enough that we refrain from harming them, but that our greater mission is to serve them. Francis was so filled with the love of

God that his own love overflowed to all species. He believed that humans and animals were all brothers and sisters under God. According to legend he would preach sermons to the animals and tame wild mice and bloodthirsty wolves. The actions of the good Saint no doubt seemed odd to the people of the time, but for Francis, it was part and parcel of his ministry. He took the words of Jesus to heart and sincerely believed that, like Christ, we are to be loving servants to the poor, the disenfranchised, and even the animals. Taking *imitatio Dei* to a whole new extreme, he was the first person in recorded history to achieve stigmata.

Many Christians who came before Francis, like many who came after him, believed that the passage in Genesis 1:26 implied superiority and exploitation. Francis took a closer look and saw that all of creation, including humans, was equally loved by God. While some theologians claim superiority by means of *imago Dei,* Francis believed that God showed himself in all, and through all, his creation. We are here to show every living animal God's love, the same way that every living animal is evidence of God's love for humanity. Both human and animals depend on God to give them life and provide for their needs. Like King Solomon in Ecclesiastes, Francis saw that animals and man are alike, both await the same fate, and both are encircled in God's own loving arms.

St. Francis had a profound impact on Christianity in general and Catholicism in particular. The Franciscan monks were founded by his then- new religious order in 1209. To this day, nearly 1000 years later, millions of people make the pilgrimage to his tomb in Assisi, Italy. In 1979, Pope John Paul II named Francis the patron saint of ecology, an act that pushed environmentalism to a more visible place within the

Church. More recently Pope Francis confirmed what roughly half of Christians already believed: that animals do, in fact, go to Heaven. The Pope, heavily influenced by the good Saint, took not only his name, but his theology as well. In 2015, he released an encyclical urging Christians to take a more environmentally sound and animal-friendly path.

16th century professor of theology, Martin Luther, famous for his 95 thesis which eventually led to the split between Protestantism and Catholicism, and founder of the church which bears his name, believed that all animals had a touch of the divine. He believed that since animals are God's creation they could serve as images for greater spiritual truths, particularly in regards to the Kingdom of God. He lamented that animals, while irrational, show compassion to the pain of their own species, yet humans, who are rational, often ignore the suffering of other humans. Luther felt a fondness towards all animals, and once reportedly told his own beloved dog to "Be thou comforted, little dog, thou too in Resurrection, shall have a little golden tail."

In 1641, Puritan minister Reverend Nathaniel Ward of the new Massachusetts Bay Colony wrote *The Bodies of Liberty* where he argued for animal sentience. He wrote that: "No man shall exercise any tyranny or cruelty toward any creature which is usually kept for man's use." This was codified into law and endorsed by the General Court. *Bodies of Liberty* was written the same year as Descartes wrote his book *Meditations*. It was no accident that at the height of Cartesian philosophy the colonies were passing laws regarding animal welfare. The Puritans, with their massive influence over New England politics, believed that the Biblical declaration of dominion meant stewardship. This wasn't unique to the colonies; they also had sway over animal rights in England.

****

The Middle Ages brought us the contrasting theology of St. Thomas Aquinas and St. Francis Assisi to Rene Descartes and Leonardo da Vinci, but to the everyday people animals were just another part of life, for better or worse. Dogs were both pets and useful tools to have around, as were other domestic animals. However, in the Middle Ages people were highly superstitious. Unfortunately, millions of animals suffered and were killed under these superstitious beliefs. It was thought that any action an animal did against a human was from the devil. It wasn't enough to kill the animal; they were actually tried and convicted in courts of law before they were sentenced to death.

In the 13th century Pope Gregory IX (1227-1241) issued a papal bull claiming that cats were of the devil. Cats, particularly black ones, were often persecuted and killed. Their owners, usually older single ladies, were tried and executed. According to NASA, light travels at 186,000 miles per second; the only thing that moves faster are rumors and urban legends. It didn't take long for the evils of cats to be exaggerated. Tall tales grew taller until cats were said to have venomous fangs, poisonous flesh, and fur that caused tuberculosis. It wasn't until the 19th century, that attitudes began to soften towards cats. After Queen Victoria, well known for her love of animals, was owned by several dogs and cats. This made cats popular again and ushered in a new age of cats as house pets. The trend continued on into the modern era. By the 1990s western nations were spending billions annually on their cats.

Despite the negative attitudes of cats in the Middle Ages, they were subject to more positive legends as well. Catholics tell the tale of the newborn baby Jesus in the stable in Bethlehem. The young infant was fussy and couldn't sleep; the new mother was at wit's end and couldn't comfort the poor child. The infant Messiah's cries attracted a stray tabby who happened by the barn. The cat jumped into the manger and snuggled up to the baby, calming him. Young Jesus, safe and warm as he snuggled the tabby, was finally able to sleep. A thankful Mary laid her hand on the cat's forehead, leaving an "M" that remains to this day.

This legend is reminiscent of the Islamic tale involving the prophet Mohammad (see page 136), and is just one of many legends surrounding cats throughout the world. Early American sailors thought that polydactyl cats (those with extra toes) were good luck and many would bring them along on ships to guarantee a safe journey. Buddhists believed that light colored cats were a predictor of silver, while dark colored predicted gold. In Celtic lore, black cats were thought to be evil, but all other cats were believed to guard the gates to the afterlife. In this regard they were the link between humans and the universe. Not surprisingly, these mixed attitudes had a profound impact on cat populations and their roles as pest control, scape goat, or pets.

Most people in the Middle Ages believed pets to be frivolous and thought that the money that would go into their care would be better served as alms for the poor. However, those with the time and money to afford them kept dogs, squirrels, birds, and to a lesser extent, cats. Most people though, put their animals to work. Dogs were guards, hunters, or herders. Most cats that were kept were pretty feral and lived in barns and used as mousers. Pigs, sheep, oxen, cattle, and chickens were as common farm animals then as they are now. Horses were mainly kept by the aristocracy, but could occasionally be found on farms.

****

The Middle Ages weren't a time of compassion and understanding. Sadly, cruelty and injustice were the norm. Women, children, and peasants had little to no rights and were often abused. The church, rather than stand as a beacon of hope and love, was steeped in corruption. Animals were often treated as harshly as everyone else. They suffered abuse in everyday life, and were tortured to death for sport. Yet while the Middle Ages brought out the worst that humanity had to offer, it also brought out the best.

16th century Puritans were horrified at the idleness and drunken revelry that accompanied the blood sports. They felt that it profaned God himself, and like St. Thomas Aquinas (see chapter 6), they believed the animal cruelty drug people down into spiritual decay. Moreover, they believed such actions were a perversion of Genesis 1; that our rule over animals meant mercy, not death. They led a reform movement that helped shape the attitudes of Western Europeans over the next few centuries.

As Europe became more modern, agricultural practices were refined and more Europeans became dependent on domestic animals. By the 1500s sheep outnumbered people 3 to 1. Peasants often shared their farmhouses with sheep and pigs. Oxen, arguably one of the most important farm animals, were too expensive for most people. It was not uncommon for villagers to split their money to share an ox or two. The animals used for livestock are the same species as now, only they tended to be smaller as they had less access to veterinary care and premium nutrition. However, by the late Middle Ages, they began to increase in size and better resemble our current livestock.

The practices and beliefs surrounding animals has evolved a lot over the earliest days of civilization through the Middle Ages and the Renaissance. While there were many variations throughout the different cultures. There were also many differences on an individual level. Some people thought that animals should be nurtured and cared for, while others thought it was our divine right to exploit them. Pets were given a great deal of care by some and used by others for sport fighting against bears, bulls, wolves and other dogs. As we evolved, so did our view of animals. This is a constant change and still today we can watch our cultural beliefs grow to better nurture the needy of all species, animal and human. Cruelty eventually led to minor reform, but it was a slow process.

CHAPTER VIII

THE INDUSTRIAL REVOLUTION

Until we extend our circle of compassion to all living things, humanity will not find peace.
-Albert Schweitzer

Many theologians and philosophers throughout the ages taught love and compassion in regards to animals. Nevertheless, Aristotelian and Cartesian philosophy and Aquinas' theology seemed to have the greater impact on the hearts and minds of the laity. Some people felt that not only was it permissible to exploit animals, but that care and compassion for them could be interpreted as a form of paganism. Man not only sought to conquer animals, but that need for conquest seeped into the entire natural world. No one can lift themselves up by pushing others down, yet the post-industrial society tried just that. Humans, not animals, were made in God's image. Therefore humanity is superior and it is our divine right to use, abuse, and kill animals.

The fact that such beliefs flew in the face of Biblical teaching was of no concern as Biblical truths are often interpreted at the reader's whim. The barbarous and exceedingly brutal practices of bear, bull, badger, and rat baiting, sport hunting, dog fighting and cockfighting continued into the 18th and 19th centuries and were considered nothing more than fun and games. Racehorses were forced to run past the point of exhaustion, sometimes running until they fell down dead on the tracks. Other popular pastimes included cock throwing, which consisted of throwing clubs at roosters until they were dead, and the aptly named fox tossing, where foxes were tossed high into the air by sling, sometimes dogs, cats, and badgers were substituted in this depraved sport.

Newspapers reported on these sports the same way that they would report on a football game. *The World*, the now defunct New York newspaper on November 28, 1883, posted an event with the headline:

A Cockfight In A Cellar
Staten Island Policemen and Judges Enjoy the Sport

Two Justices of the peace, four constables, three high officials of Richmond County and a host of other men, a majority of whom were evidently members of the short-haired fraternity, witnessed a cocking main that took place last night in a hostelry at Stapleton S.I. The pit in which the battles were fought was situated in a basement and was within easy reach of a bar that supplied the oft-repeated calls for stimulants. The conditions were that each should show seventeen birds and fight all that fell in, $50 a battle and $200 on the odd battle. The second and third battles were won by Staten Island and the first, fourth, and fifth by Connecticut.

The keen-eyed reader will notice the attendees. It wasn't young hoodlums who had gathered to watch the animals fight. The gamblers were distinguished older men. High officials, policemen, Justices of the Peace all met together to bet on which roosters would die that day. The news reported on it as a matter of fact. Why get upset? It was just another sport to be reported on.

The bloodlust of such barbarity was reminiscent of that seen at the Roman Colosseum where humans and animals alike were killed for spectacle. When mankind fell from Grace we fell hard. The curse of Adam punished the very soil we live on as we exploited the environment, animals, and people. Since animals were here for human use, few objected to the practice of trapping beautiful South American birds to slay for their plumage. Kidnapping beloved family pets to sell to vivisectionist was cruel to both the animals and their people, but for the thieves it paid very well.

Hunters would kill bears for the sole intention of stuffing them for display; people would blind their pet songbirds so that they would sing more. Cats were skinned alive for their furs. The savage practice of factory farming was in its infancy and then, as now, the masses willingly turned a blind-eye to the inhumanity within. Zoological gardens, though they date back thousands of years, became a popular fixture in almost all major cities. Unfortunately, the animals inside were ill-kept, mistreated, and died young. Proving that man can be just as callous to their own species; human zoos, inhabited by the mentally ill, were also popular attractions.

****

The Industrial Revolution brought unimaginable advances in technology, previously unseen economic opportunities, and medical advances that greatly improved the quality and quantity of life, but, sadly, much abuse came with it. Animals, the poor, women, and children were all exploited; whips and chains were the solution to the unruly of all species—including humans. The machinery of progress was fueled by the (at times literal) blood of those less fortunate and neither humans nor animals had rights to protect them. It wasn't until the 19th and 20th century that welfare began to improve for those unfortunate enough to be crushed under the boots of unshackled greed. Ironically, rights for orphans and other children came about through the newly formed American Society for the Prevention of Cruelty to Animals (ASPCA), who argued that children were an animal who deserved the same rights and protections.

While inhumanity and domination abounded during the Industrial Revolution, it was not unchallenged. From the soil of increased urbanization grew Romanticism. While many people felt that nature and wildlife were things to be conquered, romantics developed nostalgia towards a more rural way of life. The artists, intellectuals, and poets who were at the forefront of the movement felt that industrialization was inherently cruel. Among them were Ralph Waldo Emerson and Henry David Thoreau, who wrote extensively about nature and the effects it had on one's spiritual well-being.

Romantics had a profound impact on culture and politics; however, they weren't the only force striving for change. In 1833, in England, the Factory Act was passed into law declaring that children under the age of 9 could not work in any factory except silk mills. While children under 13 couldn't work more than 9 hours per day, and that children under 18 could not work more than 12 hours a day. Around the same time, unions began to make their mark on society fighting for basic rights for workers.

The new philosophy of Karl Marx in 1843 separated the bourgeoisie (land owners) from the proletariate (working class), and eventually gave rise to socialism and its cousin communism. These ideas affected the political landscape as workers demanded more political rights. The divide between capitalism and communism eventually led to conflict among the two philosophies. This escalated into wars as people on both sides died defending their ideology. Meanwhile, by the 20th century, more socialized ideas began to creep into the government and this modified form of socialism became the norm among the capitalism of Western Europe and North America.

****

The new focus on human rights brought with it an interest in animal rights. On city streets, inside coffee shops, on mission fields, inside churches and in Sunday school classrooms, the earliest animal welfare advocates could be found. In the late 18th and early 19th century, the Protestant revival, known as the first, and decades later the second, Great Awakenings were in full swing. Ministers would travel from city to city preaching the word of God, and with it, the godly ideas of social justice. Children and animals, society's most vulnerable, were believed to be in equal need of protection.

In England, 1776, while America was declaring her independence, the good Reverend Humphrey Primatt wrote *A Dissertation on the Duty Of Mercy and Sin of Cruelty to Brute Animals*. In addition to having the quintessential 18th century overly long title, the work invoked the Golden Rule that we should do to others as we would want them to do to us. Primatt wrote that animals should suffer no *"...neglect or abuse. Let no views of profit, no compliance with custom, and no fear of ridicule of the world, ever tempt thee to the least act of cruelty or injustice to any creature whatsoever."*

A couple of years later, Jeremy Bentham wrote *Introduction to the Principles of Morals and Legislation*. He argued that for too long animals have been neglected and should be legally protected. Included in that work was a tiny footnote that went on to become the rallying cry of the animal rights movement in the 20th century: "The question is not, Can they reason? Nor, Can they talk? But can they suffer?"

Meanwhile, American Minister Charles Grandison Finney (1792-1875), one of the fathers of the American Revival movement, and one of the foremost leaders of the Second Great Awakening, was an advocate for social reform. An abolitionist, he fought for both human and animal rights. In his exegesis on Christian conduct, he included mercy to animals. Finney lit a fire under his converts who fought for prison reform, women's rights, humane treatment of the mentally and physically handicapped, and the aforementioned abolition of slavery and animal welfare.

In his work; *Skeletons of a Course of Theological Lectures*, he broadened the 6th commandment; thou shalt not kill, to include animals. While he believed that it was ethical to eat animals or kill them in self-defense, he condemned the popular blood sports that were popular in the day. Finney believed that dominion meant stewardship and believed that the Biblical laws for kindness were meant to be extended to animals as well.

Finney was not the only social reformer who felt that animal welfare and abolition of slavery went hand in hand.

Many abolitionists felt that animal welfare was the litmus test for human morality. In novels, slaveholders were portrayed as animal abusers whereas abolitionists emphasize kindness and mercy to all God's creatures. These works of fiction had greater influence than the pleas of ministers and helped sway public opinion in favor of social reform.

In England, evangelical William Wilberforce (1759-1833), a Member of Parliament, and leader of the movement to end the slave trade, was also a proponent of animal welfare laws and one of the founding members of the RSPCA in 1824. As a politician and an activist, his main priority was to end the slave trade, but he was among the forerunners of the animal welfare movement. Wilberforce was a deeply religious man, he wrote *A Practical View of the Prevailing Religious System of Professed Christians in the Higher and Middle Classes in this Country, Contrasted with Real Christianity* (1779). Wilberforce condemned the popular blood sports, particularly bull baiting. He didn't confine his activism to Parliament or books. It was part of his identity; he fought cruelty in his daily life, including the very streets he walked. On one occasion he got out of his carriage and intervened when a driver was beating his horse.

****

Of course, Wilberforce was in good company in his fight for social justice. In fact, the majority of people in the United States and England who fought for the rights of all humans also fought for animal welfare. To them, it was two sides of the same coin. After the Civil War and the end of slavery, animal activism gained greater ground in both the U.S. and the U.K.

The Civil War took the lives of hundreds of thousands of people. To appreciate the societal impact that had considering the proportion to the population at the time; this would be the present day equivalent of millions of people. It devastated both the north and the south, and it would not be until the 20th century before the country would begin to see any substantial recovery. To this day, the scars on the nation have not fully healed.

People were horrified by the immeasurable cruelty of the war and renewed their focus on kindness and empathy towards all creation. Abolition gave birth to the women's rights movement, and both shared a focus with animal rights. Compassion often multiplies. The war torn and blood weary United States sought peaceful methods to achieve liberty and equality for women, and humane treatment of animals and children. Where the abolitionists fought for animal welfare prior to the civil war, suffragettes fought for animal rights after the war.

In the late 19th and early 20th century the suffragette movement fought a long and difficult, though ultimately successful, battle to secure women's rights to vote. Women's rights were at the foreground of the movement which was also deeply tied to animal rights. Frances Power Cobbe (1822-1904) was a dedicated social reformer, and if not the most important activist in the 19th century, she was certainly among the busiest. She served as an executive member of the London National Society for Women's Suffrage, promoted university degrees for women, and advocated for victims of domestic abuse.

Not one to rest on her laurels, she fought just as hard for the welfare of animals as she did the rights of women; creating both the Victoria Street Society (later renamed the National Anti-Vivisection Society) in 1875 and the British Union for the Abolition of Vivisection in 1898. Cobbe and other suffragettes in the United States and British Empire fought bitterly to ban vivisection, and their protests sometimes turned into riots as pro-vivisection medical students would oppose them at their marches and target them at their homes.

As medical science advanced, so did the use of animals in research. This led to the formation of many anti-vivisection organizations, though none, to date, have been successful in passing a complete ban. The first anti-vivisection law, the Cruelty to Animals Act, was passed in 1876 by British Parliament. This act limited, but it did not ban, animal research. It wasn't until 1966 that the United States saw similar legislation with the Animal Welfare Act. This is the only federal law in the U.S. that regulates treatment of animals. There is hope, however, as currently, the FDA is supporting the research and development of new methods to replace and eliminate animal testing.

****

The biggest social issues of the 18th, 19th, and 20th centuries were humane treatment of animals and children, rights for women, abolishing slavery, and the anti-vivisection movements. In England, decades before Finney began preaching justice for all creation, and Frances Power Cobbe fought for women and animal rights, John Wesley, father of the Methodist Church, fought for the rights of children and freedom for slaves, even as he fought for the rights of animals.

Wesley believed that animals experience suffering, sickness, and death because of the sin that entered the world after the fall of man. According to Wesley, because animals suffer by the sins of humanity, God, in all his perfection, owes salvation to the animals. In his sermon, *The General Deliverance*, he wrote that "*...something better remains after death for these poor creatures also; that these, likewise, shall one day be delivered from this bondage of corruption, and shall receive an ample amends for all their present suffering.*" He felt that while all predatory animals inflict pain on other animals, the pain humans cause them was far greater, he preached:

And what a dreadful difference is there, between what they suffer from their fellow brutes, and what they suffer from the tyrant man! The lion, the tiger, or the shark, gives them pain from mere necessity, in order to prolong their own life; and puts them out of their pain at once: But the human shark, without any such necessity, torments them of his free choice; and perhaps continues the lingering pain till, after months or years, death signs their release.

To Wesley it was unthinkable that a just God would allow such unfathomable cruelty to animals without offering a reward upon their deaths. However, as Christians, it was not enough that we be content to let animals receive justice only after they died. Wesley believed that faith in Christ would lead to better treatment to both humans and animals. Were it not for humans, animals wouldn't suffer in the first place. Therefore, we must embrace our caretaker role and become more compassionate. We must practice *imitatio Dei*, and strive to be perfect as our Heavenly Father is perfect.

Wesley preached: "When we see how much God cares for creatures, we can rest assured that God cares more for us. And because God cares for animals, we should also care for them." One of the key principles of the Methodist church is "Do all the good you can, by all the means you can, in all the ways you can, in all the places you can, at all the times you can, to all the people you can, as long as ever you can." Wesley knew that action was more powerful than words, he didn't just preach sermons, he lived his faith by action, reportedly traveling 4,000 miles annually and preaching tens of thousands of sermons.

****

Richard Martin, member of the Irish parliament, was another who lived out his faith by deeds. Martin was born into a devout Catholic family, but at the time, Catholicism in Ireland was under Protestant oppression. His father, wishing the boy to have greater opportunities, aligned him to the Church of England. The gambit paid off as it later allowed him to become a politician.

Martin was an ardent supporter of social reforms on many fronts, fighting for Catholic emancipation, abolition of slavery, and the eradication of the death penalty. He was also a hot head with a fondness for participating in duels, it is said that he fought over a hundred. Most notably for the purpose of this discussion, he fought one against a man known as "Fighting Fitzgerald" who had shot and killed an Irish Wolfhound belonging to a friend of Martin. Angry, he challenged Fitzgerald to a duel, and both men were wounded. It is rumored that Fitzgerald wore protection under his shirt which kept him from further injury.

Martin is most well-known, however, for the Cruel Treatment of Cattle Act in 1822, also known as Martin's Act. This law imposed a minimum penalty of 10 shillings to anyone who "beat, abused, or mistreated any horse, mare, gelding, mule, ass, ox, cow, heifer, steer, sheep, or other cattle." Shortly after this legislation was passed, a man named Bill Burns was caught beating his donkey.

In court, seeing that the verbal arguments against the defendant were ineffective, Martin had the donkey brought into the courtroom. The judge, upon witnessing the wounded animal, found Burns guilty. Burns was fined the minimum amount of 10 shillings, but as he was a poor man, Martin took pity on him and paid half the fine. Martin attempted to pass similar legislation against dog fighting, cock fighting, and bull baiting. He failed in that endeavor, but fortunately, a year after his death, animal fighting was included under the umbrella of the Martin Act.

****

In June of 1824, in the Olde Slaughter Coffee House on St. Martin's Lane, near Piccadilly Circus, London, Reverend Arthur Broome met with Richard Martin, William Wilberforce, Thomas Foxwell Buxton, Sir James MacKintosh, Basil Montague, John Ashley Warre, Sir James Graham, T.G. Meymott, Rev. George Bonner, Rev. George Avery Hatch, William Mudford, and Lewis Gompertz. With the exception of Gompertz, the founders were all practicing Christians whose faith shaped their activism. Three of them were Anglican Ministers. The good Reverend Broome called the meeting as he was determined that animals would see justice for their often cruel treatment.

Broome and the other gentlemen met that night to discuss ways that they could protect animals; this led to the founding of the Society for the Prevention of Cruelty to Animals. This was the world's first animal protection and welfare agency. In their first year alone, they were able to prosecute 63 offenders. In the 1830s Princess Victoria had taken an active interest in the charity. She was crowned queen in June of 1837 and in 1840, she granted royal patronage to the society. From there it became the Royal Society for the Prevention of Cruelty to Animals (RSPCA) and gained much greater influence.

Founding member of the RSPCA, Lewis Gompertz, was the only Jew among the group of Christians and this eventually led to tension among the men. This tension eventually prompted him to leave and form his own group; Animal's Friend Society. In 1824 before the formation of the RSPCA, Gompertz, a vegan, wrote the book *Moral Inquiries: on the Situation of Man and Brutes*. He believed there to be no significant difference between humans and animals. He objected to killing any living being for any reason and at a time when such concepts were unheard of, argued against taking milk and eggs from the animals which produced them.

Gompertz had a particularly soft spot for horses as they were the most visibly abused animals in London. He believed that their use was akin to slavery (which he also opposed) and dreamed of setting aside some land for emancipated horses in the English countryside. However, he was realistic enough to know that that would never actually happen. In an effort to design a conveyance that would eliminate the need for horses he designed the first bicycle prototype. His idea, which never quite caught on with the masses, had no peddles, and was powered by a hand crank.

****

Across the world, from New York, a newly married young Henry Bergh and his wife were traveling the globe on his father's inheritance. Henry and his wife spent years traveling in Europe. On a visit to Spain he went to a bullfight, perhaps it was the first time he witnessed such an event, regardless; he was horrified by the violent display. Years later, in 1863, and back in the states, President Lincoln appointed diplomat Henry Bergh to a post in the court of Czar Alexander II in St. Petersburg. While in Russia, Bergh was appalled by the everyday mistreatment of work horses. He would walk the streets and using his position of authority in the royal courts, he would confront those abusing their horses thereby preventing cruelty as it occurred.

Less than two years later, in 1865, he left his Russian post and returned stateside by way of London. While there Bergh met with the president of the RSPCA and was impressed by their work. Upon his return to New York, Bergh fought for similar legislation to protect animals. By April of 1866, he succeeded and the American Society for the Prevention of Cruelty to Animals (ASPCA) was born. Very soon after, the first laws were enacted outlawing cruelty to animals. Bergh's philanthropy didn't end with animals. In 1874, Bergh opened the New York Society for the Prevention of Cruelty to Children. The ASPCA was the first animal welfare agency in the United States, but it wouldn't be the last. Shortly after its foundation, The American Humane Association was formed, followed by hundreds of smaller organizations over the next century and a half.

In 1877 the American Humane Association was founded with the mission to end the suffering of both children and animals. Their first act was to ensure more humane treatment of farm animals, a war they are still fighting to this day. In 1889 the American Humane Education Society (AHES) was formed in Massachusetts under the leadership of George Angell. His mission was to spread humane education throughout the nation. The AHES had workers stationed all over the country and overseas in Switzerland, Greece, Turkey, Holland, France, Mexico, Cuba, and Canada.

****

The 19th century brought large scale societal changes in the hearts and minds of the populace, but quieter changes occurred during this time period too. Prior to the industrial revolution, people would live in farmhouses with their livestock. After the rise of industry and the subsequent economic boom, people were able to move their animals into barns. Though likely unacknowledged, this left a void. As we saw in chapter 6, a need for the companionship of another species is wired into our DNA.

People filled that void by allowing smaller, designated animals to remain in the house. This gave rise to the modern era of pets. These were not mere work animals here for a specific task. These animals were considered actual family members. Pets, of course, have existed since antiquity, but this current attitude towards pets was not previously seen among the peasantry. In the Middle Ages, pets were seen as a frivolous waste of money that the pious poor couldn't afford.

However, with the new economic gains brought about through the Industrial Revolution, pets, especially lapdogs, became increasingly popular among the emerging upper middle class. Lapdogs were a status symbol among the fashionable ladies of the era. They not only signified disposable income, but disposable time as well. With no lap to sit on a lapdog is just a dog. A lapdog was supposed to literally sit in the lap of the lady of the house. Because she didn't spend her days working in factories or tilling the land, she had ample time to while away the hours with her companion.

In the Middle Ages and up through the Industrial Revolution, most people held a more utilitarian view of animals, they were valued for their usefulness towards humans. Cats were phenomenal mousers, dogs were guardians, hunters, shepherds, etc., cows were food and milk, and horses were used as transportation, farm work, and sports. The people who lived and worked with the animals may have had a strong attachment to them on an individual level, but on a societal level, animals were things, mere property to be owned, like a writing desk. Legally, this is still true today, though animals tend to be held in higher regard among the populace. Over the past 200 years or so, animals came to have increased value on an emotional, rather than utilitarian, level. The line was beginning to become clearer between pets, livestock, and wildlife.

****

In the meantime, in the wild, things were looking grim. Inside, animals were being coddled. Outside, animals were being killed. North America was being populated by people who had emigrated from Europe, from countries that had been cultivated and 'civilized' for generations. On the new frontier everything was wild. Language influences perception. It wasn't nature, it was wilderness. Nature is something to be enjoyed. Wilderness is something to be conquered. Men would cut down giant sequoias because they could. They would kill grizzly bears to prove they could. Mining companies had little regard for their destructive practices. The indigenous peoples who had occupied the regions for centuries were part of the "wildness" and even the romanticism that drew people to the new land. Fish tales of bravery and boldness encouraged others to travel west and conquer and tame the new wilderness.

This came at a terrible cost. Mercury from the gold mines was dumped into the rivers. Deforestation and urbanization drastically changed the landscape. People became more dependent on fossil fuels. In England and North America, towns that were built around steel mills were enveloped in noxious gases. Researchers have found mercury levels much higher than normal in 19th century hair follicles. In 1872 acid rain was discovered. [1] In London, 1873, three days of air pollution led to the deaths of over 1,150 people. [2] Rivers and waterways were polluted with industrial waste. This led to outbreaks of cholera as people used the waters for washing and cooking.

In Genesis man was given the command to tend to the Earth and animals. Since the very beginning, we've fallen short of our task. Our caveman ancestors have successfully wiped out entire species. Our earliest ancestors were causing the extinction of megafauna and we've continued that tradition through the times of the ancient Romans to the Middle Ages, and even to this day. As far back as 6,000 BCE, humans were causing deforestation in Israel. Since the 1600s we've caused the mass extinction of thousands of species. The plants and animals that God had deemed "very good" we decided were not good enough. We've wiped out species as a matter of convenience, greed, and, in the case of early American Bison, hatred of Native Americans. Can we get any farther from the word of God than killing animals as a means to kill humans? Today thousands of species top the list of endangered and critically endangered animals. In the 21st century, at the time of this writing, seventeen species have gone extinct.

While many people during this time period sought to conquer nature in the name of progress, many more tried to preserve it. In 1849, the U.S. Department of the Interior was established, and they managed some of the first public parks. Abraham Lincoln, in 1864 signed a bill creating Yosemite Valley, the country's first state park. In 1890, John Muir, led the movement to turn it into Yosemite National Park.

In 1870, Samuel Merritt the mayor of Oakland California, financed the dam that created Lake Merritt, the first wildlife refuge in the U.S. Two years later, President Grant signed a bill to create Yellowstone National park, the first national park in the United States. 28 May 1892, John Muir founded the Sierra Club in an effort to save the earth's resources. However, some of the biggest changes came under President Theodore Roosevelt. During his eight year tenure, he converted 225 million acres of land into the U.S. Forest Service, and created

150 national forests, and 50 wildlife refuges. Real progress was made as we began to embrace our role as caretaker to the Earth.

CHAPTER IX

MODERN TRENDS

The arc of the moral universe is long, but it bends towards justice.
Dr. Martin Luther King Jr.

Dr. Martin Luther King Jr's famous quote about the arc of the moral universe appears to hold up under scrutiny, concerning all matters of social justice. By the 20th century attitudes had begun to change and people were beginning to understand the importance of preservation and protectionism. Animal advocates still fought for slaughterhouse reform and the abolishment of vivisection. At the same time, they expanded their organization to include animal use in the entertainment industry. The methods that were used on the animals were not about training them, but subduing them, and they were subject to brutal treatment. The animals were often beaten and whipped in an effort to get them to perform in unnatural ways. Animals that didn't comply were killed. Over the next century, gradually, and with much protest, laws began to pass regarding more humane treatment for animals in the entertainment industry.

While many people took their guardianship very seriously, progress was being made to save both animals and the natural world. Unfortunately, progress is slower than cold molasses. Habitat destruction and climate change resulted in extinction at rates 100 times higher than would otherwise be without human impact. Conservationists claim that we are creating an extinction event comparable to the one that wiped out the dinosaurs. (1) In 1972 president Richard Nixon felt that existing laws regarding animals were not stringent enough. He called on congress to pass better legislation regarding animal welfare. In 1973 they passed the Endangered Species Act (ESA). Tragically, this was too late for some animals, but for others it was a massive success, as some animals have thrived and been taken off the endangered list completely.

In the 1990s the island fox, from the Channel Islands in California, saw a massive drop in their population. 90% (2) of the iconic foxes lost their lives due to a canine distemper outbreak and natural predation of golden eagles. On Santa Rosa Island the fox population fell from nearly 2,000 to only fifteen. Extinction seemed imminent. By 2004 they were listed as federally endangered under the ESA. By 2016, a mere twelve years later their numbers have recovered and the foxes are no longer at risk. This is the fastest recovery in ESA history.

2016 was a good year for Californian wildlife. In addition to the recovery of the island fox, conservationists have made much progress with the endangered California condor. The California condor is a remarkable vulture. With a wingspan of nine and a half feet, it's the largest bird in North America. They were hunted to near extinction during the 20th century, and by the mid-1980s there were only a scant 22(3) birds left in existence. All the remaining birds were taken into captivity and placed into breeding programs. By 2016, their population increased to 446 total condors in the world, 276 of which have been released back into the wild. The species is still listed as endangered, but there is much reason to hope that the successful efforts of conservationists will continue on into the next decade.

ON THE FIFTH DAY

Condors aren't the only bird that is being saved by the stewards of the earth. Across the world the Hawaiian crows are making a comeback. Corvids are one of the most intelligent species of bird. Unfortunately, the Hawaiian crow is completely extinct in the wild. For thousands of years these birds thrived on Big Island, but their population was decimated by disease, predation, and farmers. The last wild Hawaiian crow died in 2002.

For more than a decade rescuers worked tirelessly to save the handful of captive crows who were saved for breeding before the last wild ones died out. Fourteen years after the crows disappeared from the wild, six captive born fledglings were released to the Pu'u Maka'ala Natural Area Preserve. Eventually, more birds will be released. (4) Hopefully, after they reach sexual maturity, the birds will begin to mate, and for the first time in decades, they will begin to breed in the wild.

From the California condor, to the Hawaiian crow, and even the legendary bald eagle (who famously recovered from the threat of extinction as well), many birds have been saved by the good overseers of the Earth. Fortunately, they aren't alone. When one moves from the air to the oceans, they can still find species who were saved by those who accepted their role as guardian. The southern sea otter is one such example. These otters are vital to the ecosystem. Their predatory role keeps the undersea life in check and helps maintain the undersea kelp forests.

These kelp forests are of enormous importance as they provide food and protection for marine animals, while at the same time capturing atmospheric carbon dioxide and helping to reduce greenhouse gases. These important otters were near extinction until 1977 when they were listed as "threatened" under the Endangered Species Act. The 18th and 19th century fur trade decimated their populations while vulnerability to oil spills and a recently reduced range size seemed to seal their fate. Their population fell to just over a thousand when they were placed on the endangered species list. Today there are just over 3,000. Should their number continue to increase at their current rate, we will see complete removal from the list over the next couple of years. (5)

Across the country on the southeast coast, the West Indian manatee is also making a comeback. When they were first placed on the endangered species list back in the 1970s there were only a few hundred left in the wild. This is especially concerning for an animal with no known natural enemies. The biggest threat to these gentle giants is habitat loss. (6) Unfortunately, they are also killed in collisions with water craft, drowned in fishnets, trap lines, or by flood control structures and canal locks. They are also often killed when they accidentally swallow fishing lines; this causes a painful and slow death for the poor unlucky creatures.

After decades of protection on the Marine Mammal Protection Act, the Endangered Species Act, and the Florida Manatee Sanctuary Act, this species is finally making a recovery. On 30 March, 2017, they were down-listed to "threatened" by the U.S. department of the Interior. Recovery plans are still in place to protect the manatees, but today there are over 6,300 in Florida alone. A milestone success for the mammals who only decades ago numbered in the hundreds.

****

The above success stories, and others like it, show what can be accomplished. As people gained greater awareness of their role in nature, they gradually began to once again embrace their caretaker role. While greater welfare efforts are happening in nature, welfare for pets began to improve as well. Cat litter was first made commercially available to the public in the 1940s. Prior to that, people used sand and ashes when necessary, but preferred to keep cats outdoors. With the introduction of clay litter, people began bringing the cats indoors. Advances in medical technology, greater variety in food, and better parasite control in the 1930s and '40s allowed pets to live longer. These advances continue to this day and cats and dogs are living longer than ever before.

By virtue of spending our lives together, pets and livestock in the past, as now, experienced the full width and breadth of humanity's cruelty and compassion. We bestow our affection, attention, and kindness to them. By providing them with food and shelter we provide for their needs and fulfill our role as guardians. Yet while we uphold the basics of the contract to provide their needs, we are also guilty of breaking said contract. Our need to dominate and exercise wonton cruelty over a weaker being is at odds with our altruism and need to give love. This is the duality of human nature we were cursed with after the fall. The whips we've previously used to train dogs were replaced with shock collars. We've replaced tethers with crates[4]. Whereas in the past we used animals as modes of transport, now they are crushed by our transportation as we fly down the road at fifty miles per hour. We keep chickens in

---

[4] Both tethers and crates can be useful training tools, but they also have much potential for abuse, and it is in this context which they are mentioned.

battery cages, pigs in gestation crates, infant cows are cramped in pens not big enough to turn around.

We test cosmetics on them, experiment on them, torture them, and inject them with deadly diseases, all in the name of "progress" and "science." Highly social rats, dogs, and other animals are isolated in cages, helpless as they witness other animals undergo the same torture to which they themselves are subjected. Over a billion animals per year are abused in this manner. Is this any kinder than the vivisection of Descartes? The only difference is that now we know beyond doubt that animals have the capacity to feel pain and experience emotions.

In the past century, hunters would kill bears to display inside their homes. It was a show of manliness that such powerful beasts could be conquered by the guns of teenage boys and young men wanting to prove their manhood. Today, wealthy grown men hunt tigers and elephants as a display of their wealth and might. The only difference between then and now is that now we know that the hunted animals are in danger of extinction. Dog and cock fighting has been outlawed, but it hasn't been eliminated. It wasn't until 2007 that cock fighting was outlawed in Louisiana, [7] making it the last state in the Union to do so.

Perhaps tellingly, it wasn't a unanimous decision. Many proponents of the blood sport fought the ban, claiming it was national heritage and tradition. With cockfighting banned in all fifty states, advocates turned their attention on the territories, particularly Puerto Rico. In response the island territory passed the Puerto Rican Gamecocks of the New Millennium Act, stating that cockfighting is a part of their cultural heritage. What this means is that now it's illegal to make cockfighting illegal. In an effort to keep the violence out of the mainland, President George W. Bush made it a federal crime to transport gamecocks across state or national borders. Nevertheless, hundreds of thousands of dollars are gambled annually in large cities by bloodthirsty crowds who thrill at the violence and destruction.

****

Dog fighting also brings in top dollar for gamblers lacking conscience and scruples. By nature, dogs are nonviolent. To build strength, endurance, and teach them violence, the criminals will chain a dog to one beam, a small animal to another and attach them both to a rotating pole in the middle. The dog runs in circles chasing the bait and at the end is rewarded with that same animal. Small animals will also be tied up as bait while the dogs maul them. Dogs are often given steroids, exercised on treadmills, [8] and kept on a large, heavy chain, often with a specially weighted harness. Losing dogs are often beaten and killed.

Contrary to popular belief, fighting dogs are not inherently aggressive, nor are they aggressive towards humans. The dominant behavioral trait in these dogs is a desire to please. Criminals exploit this good nature, and the dog's theory of mind, for their own profit and enjoyment. The criminals who run those operations will kill underperforming dogs, often with their bare hands.

In 2007, the Atlanta Falcons football player, Michael Vick, and his partners in crime; Tony Taylor, Purnell A. Peace, Oscar Allen, and Quanis L. Phillips, were caught running a large dog fighting operation named Bad Newz Kennels. [9] In

April of 2007, three dogs were hanged from trees, three were drowned in a five gallon bucket of water, and Vick and Peace personally killed a dog by repeatedly slamming him to the ground, breaking his neck and back. That was just the dogs killed in one month. Through 2002-4 Taylor, Peace, and Phillips shot and electrocuted numerous dogs who didn't "test" well.

Between 2000-2007 dogs were routinely electrocuted, beaten, hanged or shot when they underperformed or failed the test as fighters. On two occasions Vick even placed his family's pet dogs in the ring, not for gambling, but for fun. Witnesses claimed [10] that Vick and his cohorts would put family pets in the ring against the trained fighting dogs as they "...thought it was funny to watch the pit bull dogs belonging to Bad Newz Kennels injure or kill the other dogs." On June 29, 2007, fifty-three dogs were seized from Vick's Virginia property. The actions of these men are beyond reprehensible, but do bring to light the very real fights that continue in major cities all over the world. With this newfound awareness came the desire to fight it.

Michael Vick was a celebrity. Most dog fighting busts don't make the local news, let alone national. Because Vick was such a high profile person, everybody became aware that dog fighting was as popular as ever. In fact, police reported an uptick in fighting after the Vick bust. A rise, that tragically, continues to this day. Animal fighting was never gone, it had only moved underground. In 2007 it was forced out into the open, splashed across every newspaper, on the radio, T.V., and the Internet. People were forced to confront what they couldn't ignore and they were appalled.

For their parts in the crime; Phillips was sentenced to twenty-one months in prison. Peace was sentenced to eighteen months in prison, Taylor two months in prison. Allen three years' probation, and Vick twenty-three months in prison, and ordered to pay $928,073.04 for the long-term care of the pit bulls. Vick was released 20 July 2009, after serving only eighteen months. That same year, Vick signed with the Philadelphia Eagles and made $5.25 million in his first season. In 2013, he purchased a Belgian Malinois from a breeding kennel in Georgia.

In 2017 Vick retired from football and in June of that same year, he was honored in a retirement ceremony where former Falcons center Todd McClure called him the "King of Atlanta." In September 2017, Vick was hailed the "greatest Virginia Tech athlete in the school's history." He, along with five other Hokie's players, was inducted into the Virginia Tech Sports Hall of Fame. A petition against the school gathered over 150,000 signatures to prevent Vick's induction, but Virgina Tech included him nonetheless.

The real victims of the fights, the dogs, were all rescued by Best Friend's Animal Society, rehabilitated, and all but two[5] were re-homed. Some of the dogs went on to become service and therapy dogs, bringing comfort to countless people in hospitals. One dog in particular, Hector, was adopted by a Minnesotan couple, Andrew and Clara Yori, who certified him as a therapy dog. He visited nursing homes, hospitals, and even traveled to schools to teach children empathy, compassion, and safe behaviors around dogs. Unfortunately, Hector passed away from cancer in 2014. But he was able to

---

[5] As per a court order, Best Friends Sanctuary was forbidden to adopt them out, as they didn't pass the AKC's Canine Good Citizen's Test. They remain at the sanctuary where they are well-cared for.

live out his life in a happy home where good people taught him what it is like to be loved.

The rest of Vick's dogs brought joy to the people who adopted them and were able to live out their lives with the special treatment and care they deserved. They taught an entire nation about second chances. Were it not for Good Samaritans, the dogs would have been killed by the savage hands of Bad Newz Kennels. Instead, they spread happiness to the people who adopted them, while those who were therapy dogs brought healing to countless individuals.

Fortunately, further good came from the horrendous crimes of Bad Newz Kennels. Policy changed at shelters regarding dogs seized in animal fighting operations. Previously, dogs seized were immediately euthanized. Because of all the public interest in the case, the dogs seized in Vick's organization were spared. This had a lasting effect on other shelters. Now dogs are evaluated on a case by case basis and many are re-homed and given a second chance at life.

Dog fighting was changed into two histories: before Michael Vick, and after. Before Vick, laws were lenient, despite the extreme violent nature of the crimes. After Vick, laws became stricter as an angry public demanded change. Vick's fame put his crimes on the front page news. Dog fighting was forced into public discourse and people were outraged. This allowed for some positive changes regarding organized fights.

The Animal Fighting Prohibition Enforcement Act of 2007 allowed for stricter penalties against dog fighters. In 2008, Idaho and Wyoming became the last states to make dog fighting a felony offense. In 2014, US President Barack Obama signed into law the Animal Fighting Spectator Prohibition Act making it a federal offense to intentionally attend an organized fight, with added penalties for those who bring their children to such fights. In 2016, the U.S. Sentencing Commission (11) voted to make animal sentencing more strict. Previously, the average prison sentence for offenders was six months, while the majority of offenders only received probation. The new guidelines raise the sentencing to 21-27 months in jail. Drawing on the new Animal Fighting Spectator Prohibition Act, they created 6-12 month sentences for anyone who brings a child to an organized fight.

Vick is evidence of how far humanity has fallen. Abandoning our role as guardian is bad; outwardly harming animals for fun is demonic. Tragically, animal fighting is nothing new. Whereas previously it was sport enjoyed by the masses; from the peasantry to the aristocracy, today it is enjoyed only by criminals. The violent men and women of society who are more than willing to break the law for these underground games. Most people are appalled by it. Offended by the very mention of the sport, they wish to sweep it out of sight and mind. Sadly, Bad Newz Kennels wasn't the only controversy in the 20th century.

****

In 1916, in Kingsport Tennessee, Charlie Sparks, owner of Sparks World Famous Circus Show, hired a drifter named Walter "Red" Eldridge for the job of elephant trainer. Eldridge had no experience handling animals. Let alone a multi-ton animal who possesses a brain with the complexity similar to that of a human. Naturally it ended in disaster. Eldridge was given a training implement, basically a spear-like tool that he was to use to control the animal. He rode on top of an elephant named Mary during the elephant parade. Witnesses testified that he jabbed her behind the ear when she knelt down to eat a watermelon.

Mary grabbed him with her trunk and threw him off her shoulders before crushing him to death. The outraged onlookers tried to shoot her while the crowd yelled for her death. Charlie Sparks, ever the showman, felt that the best way to handle the situation would be a public execution. On September 13, 1916, Mary was transported to Erwin, Tennessee. In front of a crowd of over 2,500 people, Mary was led to a railway yard which served as her makeshift gallows. Witness Myrtle Taylor [12] recalled that every kid in the county was there that day. Mary was followed by the circus's other four elephants, led as if they were in a parade, to bear witness to her death.

Elephants, of course, are highly emotional and extremely social animals. Their presence at Mary's hanging was emotionally cruel to them, but Sparks thought they would keep Mary calm. Unfortunately, that wasn't the case. They called out to Mary, and to keep her from running away, one of her legs was tethered to a rail. That was a bad idea on top of all the other bad ideas that led up to that moment.

As she was lifted up, her bones and ligaments snapped, the chain around her neck broke, and she fell five feet to the ground breaking her hip. They tried again, as the bloodthirsty crowd of men, women, and children, laughed and cheered. She hung there for thirty minutes before she died. After she was lowered into her grave, a veterinarian performed a necropsy and found that she had a badly infected tooth in the same area that Eldridge had prodded her.

The life and death of Mary is surrounded by folklore and legend. The above account is a composite of what happened, drawn from multiple sources, as eyewitnesses are long dead by now. At the time, Mary's execution was spectacle. Sadly, it wasn't the only, or even the first, of its kind. On January 4, 1903, a circus elephant named Topsy was fed carrots laced with cyanide, had a rope placed around her neck, and electrodes around her feet, and was killed by the combination of poison, strangulation, and electrocution. The plan was to hang her, but the ASPCA stepped in and prevented that as it was considered too inhumane.

Topsy was born a free elephant in 1875, in Southeast Asia but was captured as an infant by elephant traders and sold to Forepaugh Circus. In 1902 a drunk spectator named James Fielding Blount wandered over to the elephant tent and began teasing them and offering them whiskey. Blount allegedly burnt the tip of Topsy's trunk with his cigar so she threw him to the ground and crushed him to death. Word soon spread about the 'killer elephant' and crowds came in droves to watch her. Six months after the death of James Blount, a spectator named Louis Dodero poked her ears with a stick. She picked him up with her trunk and threw him to the ground but her handler William Alt, intervened before she did any further harm.

The attack on Dodero prompted the owners of Forepaugh Circus to sell her to Sea Lion Park, later sold and renamed Luna Park by new owners. William Alt came along with Topsy and both helped out as the new Luna Park moved to a larger location. In October, a drunk William Alt was unsuccessful at getting Topsy to move an amusement ride, so he stabbed her with a pitchfork. Alt was immediately confronted by police so he released Topsy and she ran the streets of Coney Island. Alt was arrested for the incident. In December, drunk again, Alt rode Topsy through the streets of Coney Island to the police station. There, Alt used her to try to batter the station door while the terrorized police hid in the cells.

After that stunt, Luna Park fired Alt and tried to sell Topsy. There were no buyers, so the Park's owners, Frederick Thompson and Elmer Dundy, decided to just kill her instead. Their plan was to hang her and charge admission, but when the ASPCA objected to that idea they considered other methods to end her life before settling on electrocution and poison. Unlike Mary's tragic and brutal death, Topsy was killed in a matter of seconds. This proved that electrocution was a humane method of execution and eventually led to its use as capital punishment on human criminals, replacing the gallows.

The generator used was Edison Electric Illuminating Co, and the event was filmed by Edison Manufacturing Co. The film is a 74 second documentary filmed by Edwin Porter and is available online. Despite popular myth, Thomas Edison [13] himself had nothing to do with the murder, nor was he present when it happened. While Edison was nowhere near the grisly spectacle, that didn't stop an estimated 1500 people from coming for the show, though only 100 were allowed into the park.

The two unfortunate elephants' deaths drew large crowds as people desperate for entertainment flocked the streets. At the turn of the century many people didn't consider animal life to hold any value. Today, people are appalled by the deaths of Mary and Topsy. These stories show how far attitudes have changed over the decades. In the past animals were disposable. Over the last few centuries as activists fought for the rights of animals, they faced constant opposition and derision by those who are eager to shirk their role as caretaker. While this is still true today, overall, humans are getting better in regards to animals.

****

There is much reason to be optimistic about the future of animals. Though humanity has often been guilty of rejecting the role of guardian, there are those who've accepted that mantle of responsibility. Many people throughout the ages have worked tirelessly to save and protect the animals and the Earth. When people began to draw more than they needed from the Earth's resources the Earth and all its inhabitants suffered. However, this raised awareness of how important clean air, potable water, and abundant wildlife are to the Earth.

This resulted in many positive changes; the Vegetarian Society was founded in Britain in 1847. Different countries have developed systems of national parks. The Audubon Society was founded in New York in 1905 to protect wild birds. The Humane Slaughter Act was passed in the United States in 1958. In 1964, federal legislation passed the Wilderness Act, soon to be followed by the National Wild and Scenic Rivers Act and the National Trails Act. In 1992, representatives from over 170 countries meet in Brazil to attend the United Nations Conference, known as Earth Summit with the goal to create a global consensus on ecological matters. That same year, Switzerland became the first country to provide legal protection for animals in its constitution. A decade later, in 2002, Germany followed suit.

In 1986 the International Whaling Commission (IWC) issued a moratorium on commercial whaling. Iceland and Norway have officially objected to the ban and continue to hunt whales. Japan, in defiance of the ban, and despite global criticism, also continues the practice of whaling. In 2017, they killed 333 (14) minke whales, an action which was condemned by the International Court of Justice.

In 2011, Japan suffered a devastating magnitude nine earthquake, whose effects were felt around the world. This unleashed a powerful tsunami, causing further damage to a broken country. Nearly 16,000 people were killed, the majority of whom drowned. The damage from the disasters is an estimated $300 billion (US dollars), as of this writing, the country still suffers from the effects of the quake and the damage done to its nuclear plant. Stunned, the global community pitched in, donating $230 billion in aid. Imagine the outrage, then, when Japan used nearly $30 million in donations earmarked for earthquake recovery to fund their annual whale hunt. They returned from their hunt (which they dub "research") with 900 whales. This sparked global outcry amongst the public.

Despite these outliers, the IWC has actually been a tremendous success. Whaling was a giant industry in the 18th and 19th century. It continued on into the 20th century, losing ground only when the IWC was formed in the 1960s. For the first several years the IWC was not very effective. That is, until, the mid-1980s. The moratorium drastically reduced hunting and brought nearly every single species of whale back from the brink of extinction.

During the heyday of ocean hunting, between the turn of the century and 1966, 90% of humpback whales were killed. It was predicted that they would be extinct by the new millennium. When the IWC ban was enacted in 1986, there were only 5,000 humpback whales in existence. After the ban, the numbers soared. This is remarkable considering that they don't produce as many offspring as other mammals. Today there are approximately 80,000 humpbacks and their numbers are continuing to increase. The IWC [15] estimates their rate of increase to be 83.2% per year. While they still face human-made threats in the wild (net entanglement, ship strikes, and environmental dangers), hunting, for the most part, is no longer one of them.

Perhaps the most famously hunted of all animals was the bison. They nearly went extinct in the 19th century by settlers who thought it was their divine right to move west and 'civilize' the new country. Hunters shot the bison from passing trains, drove them off cliffs, or simply slaughtered their herds as they came across them. Anywhere between 30 to 60 million bison once crossed the North American plains, a number that fell to just 325 in the 1800s. Today roughly 500,000 [16] live in North America, and fewer than 30,000 roam free in conservation herds. Wood Buffalo National Park has approximately 10,000 wood bison, making it the largest population of the once endangered animal. Bison are considered near threatened, but have a steady population with many conservation programs protecting them.

****

There are numerous wildlife success stories in recent decades as humanity recognizes its role as caretaker. Fortunately, animals aren't the only ones benefitting from our stewardship. In 2014, the Convention on Biological Diversity (17) adopted the Aichi Biodiversity Target 11; a multi-pronged approach to expand protected land by 17% and protected coastal and marine areas by 10% by 2020. They aim to decrease the loss of natural habitats by half, with an eventual goal of bringing the number to zero. By 2016, the protected areas saw increased expansion, particularly in the oceans. Efforts are underway to connect isolated tracts of habitat to form one large interconnected area in India, Sumatra, Ecuador, Brazil, and Colombia. Should they achieve their eventual goals, over three quarters of threatened species would receive better protection through increased biodiversity.

In addition to the Aichi Biodiversity Target 11, marine species are also being protected by Marine Protected Areas (MPAs). In 2014 several new MPAs were added to provide sanctuary to flora and fauna. Meanwhile, U.S. President Barack Obama expanded the Pacific Remote Islands National Marine Monument (one of the largest MPAs in the world) from 87,000 square miles to 490,000. Commercial fishing and energy exploration are now banned from this area. This will provide a safe space for fish to reproduce and marine flora to recover.

****

While conservation efforts are far from perfect, things are definitely improving as we grow to understand more about the world around us. We live in the Information Age. At any given moment most people can reach into their pockets, pull out their phone and do a quick internet search on any given topic. Five minutes on your favorite search engine will pull up results on Jaak Panksepp's (5 June 1943 — 18 April 2017) research on neurobiology. Or if you'd rather, you can watch videos of him tickle rats as they run around and laugh. You can also read all about the MRI studies they did on dogs and find out how our best friends really feel about us. At any given time, on any given day, someone right now is learning how emotional and intelligent animals are. Skeptics remain, but they are a slowly dying breed. As people spend more time with their pets they grow ever closer to them. As more studies are conducted, we learn more about how special they are. With that awareness comes greater responsibility. Now, more than ever, we are embracing our God-given role as caretaker.

There are more animal charities now than ever before in history. Sadly, that's because there's a need for it. The first dog pounds in the 19th Century existed as a way to get dirty dogs off the streets. The dogs were captured and killed. Today the goal is not to kill them, but to re-home them. Spay and neuter education efforts and charities have drastically reduced the number of pets in shelters since the 1990s. Animals as diverse as rabbits and reptiles and as common as cats and dogs find their way in and out of shelters as people alternately abandon and embrace their guardianship role. A Harris poll conducted in 2011 [18] found that 62% of Americans have one or more pets inside their home. Almost every single one of them, 95%, consider them a member of their family, with 71% letting the pet sleep in the bed with them. It is estimated that in 2017, 69.36 billion [19] dollars will be spent on pets.

****

In the past, religious leaders have been at the forefront of the animal rights movement. There have been naysayers, some of whom have been very loud and vocal, who argued that animals don't have souls, and are not worth any moral concern. However, many leading Christians, guided by the Bible, and God's obvious love for the world, have treated animals with compassion. Saints Antony of Padua and Francis of Assisi have both preached to animals. A pig followed St. Anthony Abbot everywhere after he cured him of an illness.

Horses knelt by St. Francis Jerome when he preached, and Saint Francis of Paola is said to have resurrected a pet lamb and two pet fish. St. Roch, the patron saint of dogs, had food brought to him by dogs when he was sick and stuck in the woods. In fact, over fifty saints in the history of Christianity have aided or been aided by animals, preached to them, resurrected them, or had other miraculous events surrounding them. Of course, this should surprise no one. Many great figures in the Bible can boast the same.

In 1990 Pope John Paul II said that animals have souls, or the 'breath of life'. As they were created by God they deserve our respect, and will join us in heaven when they die. Currently Pope Francis has embraced the concept of *imitatio Dei* and strives to live the words of Jesus: preaching to the poor and vulnerable. He once stated "Nowadays we must forcibly reject the notion that our being created in God's image and given dominion over the Earth justified absolute domination over other creatures." Francis wrote in Laudato si (24 May 2015) that our dominion is responsible stewardship.

Everything on Earth has its place and is of enormous value to God in its own right. Destruction of the environment and extinction of plant and animal species is an extremely serious offense against God.

At the forefront of the modern Christian animal rights movement is British theologian Andrew Linzey. Linzey rejects utilitarian ideas that animals are resources or human property. Animals, as creatures of God, are precious in the sight of the Lord. Linzey believes that Christian theology can provide the basis for animal rights. Since animal life is a gift from God, it is a violation against God when we endanger his creation. When we begin to look at creation from God's own point of view we can begin to feel more respect for all life.

Many churches are beginning to add pet ministries to their programs. The leaders of these churches recognize that the love between people and their pets is strong, so they seek to foster that bond. They recognize the Biblical truths that God's love pours out over the entirety of his creation. Many churches have a day set aside in October for a blessing of the pets. The Humane Society of the United States began to partner with churches in 2007 in their Faith Outreach Program. Animal ministries donate to shelters, host adoption events and run food drives. Organizations like C.A.R.E. (Christian Animal Rights Effort), A.C.C. (Animal Cristian Concern, pronounced Assisi), the ASWA (Anglican Society for the Welfare of Animals), and the Catholic Concern for Animals, are just a sampling of charities that live out their faith in action as they work for the good of others.

Though there are naysayers who reject Biblical claims of animal worth, they are increasingly being drowned out by those who acknowledge their role as caretaker over the Earth.

Very few Christians anymore believe that nature exists only to serve us, but rather we exist to serve nature. Christ instructed us to care for the weak and act with mercy and love. Therefore it is not merely something that we should, maybe do, if we want to. Rather, loving kindness is something we were commanded to do throughout the Bible.

We are entering a new era, one where through scientific advances, and Biblical research, we are recognizing the inherent worth of all God's creation. Christians can either lead the way on animal rights, or lag behind. In the 18th and 19th centuries religious leaders were on the frontline in the fight for social justice for humans and animals. They may have lagged a bit in the 20th century, but since the 1960s, once again, they're in their battle stations, along with many secular organizations, fighting for animal welfare and the environment.

CHAPTER X

PSYCHOLOGY BEHIND THE BOND

The wolf will live with the lamb, the leopard will lie down with the goat, the calf and the lion, and the yearling together; and a little child will lead them.
-Isaiah 11:6

Between observational field studies and Biblical teachings, we can safely reject the notion that animals were put here solely for human use. God clearly intended harmony in His original vision for the world. While animals are valuable in their own right, when we embrace our position as guardian we find that there are many benefits to the physical and mental well-being of both humans and animals. We may not need science to tell us that animals have a relaxing effect on people. Any person who has ever belonged to a pet can tell you how relaxing it feels to stroke a cat or pet a dog. Current research is finally affirming what lay people knew all along; pets are emotional beings who bring us great comfort. This is no accident. God, in His wisdom, created life on Earth with the idea that all live together in peace. Is it any surprise that He hard wired our brains to enjoy the company of our fellow creatures?

We live in a time when we are blessed enough to have the disposable time and money to care for animals. At least in the western world, more and more people are sharing their homes with various pets. Increasingly popular are aquariums, both the large ones that charge admission and the small in-home ones that people set up for themselves. This is not new; fish have been kept since antiquity, only now we have the means to better care for them. Popular hobbies are snorkeling and diving, people are equipping themselves to go down into water and swim with the fish. This goes well beyond the aesthetic qualities of the fish. People are drawn to fish and to the water on a much deeper level. The sound of water and the simple act of watching fish have a calming effect on people.

Researchers [1] have found that watching the light shimmer through the water and observing the biodiversity of fish had a noticeable effect on people's blood pressure and heart rates. For years, dentists and therapists have kept stocked tanks in their waiting rooms. They had recognized the calming effect that the aquariums had provided for their patients. Perhaps it is a left over memory from Eden, but it is ingrained in us to find that nature restores us and calms our souls.

Aquariums bring that bit of nature indoors. The above study found that just 10 minutes in front of a tank has been shown to improve moods and provide the observers with a more positive outlook. The more fish in an aquarium, the more that people relaxed and their moods improved. It should be noted however, that the study was conducted on a 550,000 liter tank. Most people are not able to fit a tank of that size into their living room.

Another study [2] found that fish and other animals can provide relief to the elderly in nursing homes. This trial, led by E. Paul and Ariella Cherniak, found that older people with dementia benefited from exposure to a fish tank placed in the dining area. Compared to the control group, residents were more likely to socialize and less likely to show signs of agitation. Other animals have been shown to have a positive effect on nursing home residents as well. Possibly due to the distraction they provide, possibly due to the changes in brain chemistry they provide, or possibly due to the prosocial behavior they promote. Pets have been shown to provide a net benefit to people of all age groups.

That benefit extends not only to a person's quality of life, but also effects the quantity. Researchers (3) who published a study in 1980 found that among men who had had heart attacks, those with pets lived longer on average than those without. The Centers for Disease Control and Prevention has found that people with pets typically have lower blood pressure and cholesterol which can decrease the risk of a heart attack. In 2009, Deborah Wells published *The Effects of Animals on Human Health and Well-Being.* She explored the evidence that pets enhance the health of their people, and also discussed the ways that animals, usually dogs, can detect certain diseases such as cancer, epilepsy, migraines, and diabetes.

Different chemicals are released by malignant tissue when compared to normal tissue. Animals, usually dogs, with their keen sense of smell can easily detect the difference. Dogs have 220 million smell receptors, and an olfactory bulb that puts ours to shame. It would actually be more surprising if they didn't smell cancer. And of course, cats have also been known to sniff out malignant cells and alert their people to changes.

When they tested animals against machinery (4) in 2011, a Labrador retriever was able to identify, with 97% accuracy, stool samples from patients with colon cancer. As of the time of this writing, dogs are more accurate than our best machinery. But don't neglect your yearly exams. Simply because your dog can smell cancer doesn't mean he knows how to warn you, or that you'll notice his signals when he does.

Cancer, of course, is not the only chemical your dog can detect. Animals can also detect changes in blood sugar. There are organizations that will place service dogs with diabetics. These dogs will alert their people when their blood sugar changes which gives them plenty of time to test their blood sugar and take their insulin. A study published in 2013 [5] showed that every single client in the study reported a higher quality of life with fewer unconscious episodes and paramedic visits.

****

God did not just create humans and lay us on a planet with no plants or animals. If He wanted to do that we'd all live on a Mars type planet right now and have a completely different experience. God saw fit to place us in a world teeming with life. The Bible tells us that this variety brings pleasure to God. As a species, we finally understand how they give pleasure to us too. When we look at an animal our brain is firing. Animals have been found to have a profound effect on our brain's biochemistry; they also provide a lower heart rate, lower blood pressure, and reduced stress. Not only do we experience these benefits when we pet animals, but the simple act of social gazing provides elevated oxytocin levels in our brains.

Oxytocin is a hormone made in the hypothalamus, a section of the forebrain, and it acts as both a hormone and a neurotransmitter. It effects behavior, love, and even plays a part in reproduction. Oxytocin is released during sex, when women are in childbirth, and when they breastfeed, creating a stronger bond between mother and child. This hormone also has an effect on social behavior, having a natural anti-anxiety effect. Oxytocin strengthens social memory; however, this can be a double edged sword as it can pull up bad memories along with the pleasant ones. It also increases empathy, romantic feelings, and love. It has been found that romantic partners in the first six months of a relationship have an increase in oxytocin. Some people have even referred to it as the 'love hormone.'

One study, [6] on oxytocin levels and pets, figuring that work was a common stressor, tested ten men and ten women, with and without dogs, after they returned from work. Those who had dogs were tested with them; those without dogs were given nonfiction reading materials. The subjects were tested before they saw their dogs and then retested after spending twenty-five minutes with the dogs. Those in the reading group followed the same protocol except with reading materials instead of dogs.

Interestingly, there was a difference in the oxytocin levels in the men and women. In men the oxytocin levels decreased both after spending time with their dogs and after reading. Whereas for the women, oxytocin increased significantly more for those in the dog group compared to those in the reading group. Though further study will be required, this does suggest that men and women have different hormonal responses to their pet dogs. It may indicate that petting a dog is more relaxing for women than it is for men. Or it may simply be the different effects that testosterone and estrogen have on people. More information is sure to come to light upon further examination.

Oxytocin release isn't the only chemical to be effected when we are with animals. The brain is a highly complex organ and oxytocin is just a small part of it. Many other factors are involved with human-animal interactions. Animals have also been found to affect our serotonin levels. Serotonin is produced by nerve cells and found mainly in the digestive system and helps with digestion, eating, and sleeping. It has been found to, among other things, reduce depression, heal wounds, and regulate anxiety. (7)

One study (8) from the University of Missouri-Columbia found that serotonin levels show substantial increase after interaction with animals. This study paired two groups of people with either a live dog or a robot dog and then compared blood samples. In the group who interacted with the live dogs they saw a dramatic increase in the serotonin levels, and also in prolactin and oxytocin levels. The group who played with the robot dog actually saw a decrease in serotonin.

In addition to serotonin and oxytocin; beta-endorphin, prolactin, beta-phenylethlamine, and dopamine have all increased in both dogs and humans after only thirty minutes of friendly interaction. What this means to us is that animals, specifically dogs since that is the most tested animal, cause multiple parts of our brain to react in positive ways. This ends up having a positive effect on our physical, mental, and emotional health. This provides a glimpse of God's original design.

God made our brains react in such a way that it actually improves our total body health to be in nature and around animals. Beta-endorphin is a natural pain killer; dopamine controls the brain's pleasure center. We were all built to feel mutual affection for each other. If Eden was an historical location, and had we remained there, we would be in a positive feedback loop with animals and the natural world all the time.

Out of all the animals, dogs are the only ones who bond more strongly to humans than they do to their own species. [9] This gives us a taste of the fellowship we lost in Eden. Were it not for the sins of Adam we could have had that same communion with all the animals; lions, polar bears, panthers, etc. There would be no distinction between domestic and wild, they would all be tame. As it stands, we greatly benefit when we are in nature and around animals. That is no accident.

God wants us to enjoy His creation. Not only does it provide a net positive effect on humans, but on the animals and the environment as well. When we take care not to harm the Earth, when we take our guardianship seriously, we all begin to heal. The chemical effects we feel in our brains as we interact with animals are also experienced by those same animals. Pets normalize our brain chemistry just as we normalize theirs. We were made for each other and the Bible tells us that God delights in our relationship.

Bonding created by social gazing doesn't just help humans. We share the positive effects with dogs and other animals. A study [10] found elevated oxytocin levels in dogs, but not wolves, when engaging in gazing behavior. There was no difference in oxytocin levels between different breeds or sexes of dogs. This study suggests that it was social gazing behavior that may have triggered the domestication process. It also shows that the human-dog bond is mutually beneficial and demonstrates the existence of cross-species bonding. The latter is something that most pet people didn't require proof, they already felt the bond.

Humans and dogs aren't the only ones benefiting from cross-species bonds. A sample [11] from an animal refuge in Arkansas found that play between a terrier and a goat caused a 48% increase in oxytocin in the dog. This indicates that the dog viewed the goat as his friend. However, there was a whopping 210% increase in the oxytocin levels of the goat. While studies on oxytocin levels among different animals are few and far between, they have found that cats also experience a boost in oxytocin when they are around their people. It will be interesting to see the results of future studies on this subject, but in the meantime, it is nice to know that various animals benefit from cross-species interactions.

****

We are drawn to nature and to animals. Their very presence brings out prosocial behavior among humans. Studies [12] have shown that children on the autism spectrum and children with developmental disorders are more playful in the presence of a dog, compared to toys, and more aware of their social environment. Further studies with children on the spectrum have shown that the children in the presence of a dog display greater language use. Both dogs and exposure to therapeutic riding has led to more motivation for social interaction in children with autism. Other research has found that adults in wheelchairs receive more positive interactions from strangers when they are with a service dog, compared to those without a dog.

Studies also show that everyday families, who get a dog, in as little as a month, spend more time together and have friends visit more often. Research has shown that people are more trusting of strangers when there are dogs around, compared to when they're not. And finally, studies indicate that the presence of animals has been correlated with an increase in empathy and a decrease in aggression. In adults and children, both neurotypical and those with mental health issues, contact with animals leads to better social functioning and increases trust towards other humans.

Adults and children are also able to learn compassion from animals. Research [13] has shown that while dehumanizing animals will lead to dehumanizing humans, the reverse is also true. People who humanize animals will humanize other humans. When people equate animals with humans it expands their moral concern; not just for the animals, but for humans as well. However, when people equate humans with animals it has the opposite effect. This is particularly evident in treatment of immigrants. People who show a greater concern for animal welfare are more likely to show greater concern towards immigrants.

****

We can easily see the positive effect that animals and people have on each other. We all thrive under the human animal bond. Unfortunately, we live in a fallen world. Sometimes something goes terribly wrong with that bond. The average person, who is not an animal lover, is at worst, indifferent to animals. They have no desire to interact with them, but at the same time, they wish them no harm. Tragically, this isn't always the case.

Early in history people have noticed a link between those who harm animals and the likelihood that those same people will harm other human beings. Thomas Aquinas, (pages 138-139) Immanuel Kant, and John Locke have all noticed a correlation between animal abuse and cruelty to humans. John Locke (1632-1704) wrote that *"The custom of tormenting and killing of beasts will, by degrees, harden their minds even towards men; and they who delight in the suffering and destruction of inferior creatures, will not be apt to be very compassionate or benign to those of their own kind."* A sentiment not dissimilar to the philosophy of Kant (1724-1804) who stated that *"He who is cruel to animals becomes hard also in his dealings with men. We can judge the heart of a man by his treatment of animals."*

Tragically, we don't have to look far to find this evidenced in real life. The notorious serial killer, Jeffrey Dahmer [14] was overly fascinated with animal corpses and experimentation. He got his start experimenting on road kill, and eventually he began killing animals himself. In 1975, the head of a dog was found on Dahmer's property, impaled on a stick. It should be no surprise that he eventually killed seventeen men and boys between 1978 and his capture in 1991.

Violence against animals is one of the main predictors of violence against humans. Adults are five times more likely to commit acts of violence against people if they acted violently towards animals as children or adolescents. [15] Research in Australia has shown that 100% of sexual predators had a history of violence towards animals. [16] Boston Strangler, Albert DeSalvo, would trap animals as a child and shoot arrows through them. He and a friend would also lock dogs and cats side by side in orange crates and leave them without food or water for several days. When they would finally release the animals he would watch as the confused cat redirected and attacked the dog. He grew up and refocused his violence towards women. He raped and killed 13 women, who were between the ages of nineteen and eighty-five, over an eighteen month period. DeSalvo was killed in prison in 1973 while serving out a life sentence.

The BTK killer, Dennis Rader, killed ten people in Wichita, Kansas between 1974 and 1991. He was arrested in 2005. He gave himself the BTK moniker, short for Bind, Torture, and Kill. Rader was in constant contact with the press and got a sexual thrill from the panic that gripped the city. In the end, it was his ego and naivety that ultimately led to his arrest. Rader wanted his crimes to be known so he contacted the police department offering them a floppy disc of his crimes. He asked the police if the disc could be traced asking them to "Be honest." They weren't honest and told him "no." Through that disc they were finally able to capture him, more than a dacade after his last murder.

As a teenager Rader had fantasies about sexual bondage. As a young man in the Air Force he would hire prostitutes, though none would let him live out his fantasies. While still a teenager, he began torturing and hanging dogs and cats. As an adult he took a job as an animal control officer. It was in this capacity that he would drive down streets stalking victims. According to at least one witness, he also abused his position as dog catcher and shot a dog right in front of the dog's guardians.

In his book *Whoever Fights Monsters: My Twenty Years Tracking Serial Killers for the FBI*, Robert Ressler wrote that the notorious serial killer, David "Son of Sam" Berkowitz, would spear his adoptive mother's fish with a pin and pour ammonia in the fish tank to kill them. For the thrill of watching him die slowly, and to watch his mother suffer, he killed her pet bird with rat poison. He enjoyed the helplessness his mother felt at not being able to help the bird. He was around six or seven at the time. He would torture and kill small mammals and moths, reveling in the power and control he had over their lives.

The "co-ed killer," Edmund Kemper, was often locked in the basement for long periods of time as a child. It was in that setting that he killed the family cats; one he buried alive, one he killed with a pocket knife. After running away from home and eventually moving in with his grandparents he began killing small birds. At fifteen, he killed his grandmother after she tried to remove his gun. Fearing that his grandfather would be angry with him if he found out, he killed his grandfather in the driveway as he returned home from work.

For these crimes, Kemper served a few years in juvenile hall, and was then released, his record expunged. As a young man he killed young women as practice for his ultimate goal; his abusive mother. After killing her and her friend, he turned himself into the police. A life of violence starting with the murder of animals and ending in matricide, yet another link in the chain of violence.

Robert Ressler and John Douglas, of the Behavioral Sciences Unit of the FBI, brought the field of psychiatry into the evidence and forensics based world of investigation. They interviewed 36 incarcerated serial killers and found that more than half of them committed violence against animals when they were children, and almost half had continued that violence into adolescence. Ressler and Douglas believe that these criminals had violent fantasies that they acted out on animals before graduating to humans. Ressler has said that "Murderers ...very often start out by killing and torturing animals as kids." (17) While Douglas has confirmed that the worst offenders' often began as children torturing and killing pets or wildlife.

Douglas also noted that school shooters often committed cruelty to animals before redirecting their aggression on classmates. Sadly, that appears to be a common theme. Eric Harris and Dylan Klebold bragged to their classmates about mutilating animals just a few days before they walked into Columbine High School and killed twelve students. Kipland Kinkel, known as Kip, brought a pipe bomb to school and gave a speech about how to build one. He bragged that he had blown up a cow and beheaded his cat. On May 21, 1998 he murdered both his parents and, armed with two hunting knives, two pistols, and a rifle, he walked into Thurston High school, where he was a freshman. Two students were killed in his rampage and 23 others were wounded.

17 year old, Luke Woodham wrote in his diary (18) about his "first kill." He and a friend had been beating his dog Sparkle for a while. On 14 April, 1997, after his parents had made a vet appointment for poor Sparkle, Woodham and his accomplice tied her up, put her in a book bag and beat her to listen to her "almost human" howls. Then he lit the bag on fire and continued to beat the poor girl as she burned, before throwing her and the bag into a pond to watch it sink, describing the incident in his diary as "true beauty." Is it any wonder that on

that same year on the first of October that the monster beat and stabbed his mother before driving to his Mississippi school and killing his ex-girlfriend, her friend, and then wounding seven others?

The worst school massacre in the history of the United States occurred in 1927 in Bath, Michigan. A small town of only 300 people, the school itself actually had a larger population than the village. Students from the entire region attended the Bath Consolidated School giving it a student body of 314 children and teenagers. In small-town America everybody knew each other, and everyone knew something was off about school board member and local electrician, Andrew Kehoe. Witnesses had seen him kill a neighbor's dog, beat his own horse to death, and treat his livestock poorly.

Planning for months in advance, Kehoe had planted nearly 1,000 pounds of dynamite in and around the Bath school building. On the last day of school, May 18, the hundreds of pounds of dynamite in the school's basement erupted with such force that the explosion was heard several miles away. Firemen later found an additional 500 pounds that never detonated. The blast left piles of children beneath the rubble. It wasn't until 6:00 that night that the last child was removed from the wreckage.

While the community pitched in to help remove the debris and rescue the children, Kehoe pulled up in his old pickup truck. The truck was filled to the brim with dynamite which he ignited killing himself, the school superintendent, and many bystanders. Earlier that day, at the Kehoe farm, Andrew had murdered his wife and two of their horses, before blowing up his own house. When the fire department arrived at his farm they found a sign attached to a fence that read "Criminals are made, not born." (19) All told, the death count came to forty-four people, thirty-eight of whom were students and the majority were only between six and eight years old.

Kehoe hated taxes and blamed the increased taxes levied to help pay for the school on the imminent foreclosure of his farm. In 1927 there was much still to learn about mental health. The community struggled to understand what would lead to such madness. A year later, the school was rebuilt and the world moved on. The school was eventually demolished nearly fifty years later and converted into a memorial park. Today, nearly one hundred years later, the world has forgotten the victims of the nation's deadliest school massacre.

****

All his research and all his interviews have led Robert Ressler to stress in *Whoever Fights Monsters* that "nobody wakes up at the age of thirty-five and decides to become a serial killer." The behaviors that lead to murder begin to develop during childhood. From birth to age six or seven, the most important person in a child's life is the mother. From her he learns how to love. Parents teach their children kindness and empathy. Parents teach their children not to pull the tail of a dog or grab a cat by the ears. Through emotional neglect and without guidance, socialization, and proper training, the children never learn to view the world in a way that is not egocentric. Even if the mother is loving and nurturing, if the father is physically or sexually abusive, the love of a mother won't be enough to prevent psychiatric harm.

Numerous reports show a correlation between spousal and child abuse and animal abuse. There is ample evidence to support animal abuse as one of many of the main predictors of family violence. In fact, animal abuse is highest in families with severe child and partner abuse. Mostly it is used as a means of control and intimidation; threats to kill the pet if the partner leaves are common, in some cases the partner actually delivers on the threat. These threats are a form of manipulation by abusers seeking to silence their victims. In some cases it is investigations into animal abuse that alerts authorities to the acts of domestic abuse within the same household.

Victims of violence often use their pets as a source of comfort and support. Witnessing violence against them causes extreme emotional trauma, especially for children who have no other means of support. This gives the perpetrator a psychological edge. Other times the abuse is by the victim as they lash out and try to assert their own control on a weaker victim. This seems to especially be the case in young boys who have experienced physical and sexual abuse.

With children it seems to be that the violence is oftentimes a learned behavior as they've witnessed the abuse of both humans and pets. Research [20] conducted in 1996 between convicted felons and university students found that nearly 2/3 of the men studied had witnessed animal cruelty in some form. Men who had been exposed to violence against animals before the age of thirteen were more likely to commit acts of violence and delinquency later in life, compared to men who haven't witnessed such acts. Observing such acts of violence can become the link in what is known as the intergenerational cycle of violence.

****

A parent is a child's first teacher. While the above examples are what can go horribly, horribly wrong, they are, thankfully, very rare. Most parents aren't emotionally, physically, or sexually abusive. The overwhelmingly vast majority of children don't grow up to be serial killers. In fact, while animal cruelty at a young age is a predictor of violence in adults, the opposite is also true. Many studies show that being attached to pets at a young age can teach affection, respect, empathy, and prosocial interhuman relationships. Taking care of an animal and being actively involved in their well-being teaches empathy and respect for those who are weaker or more vulnerable. And where violence towards animals is often a predictor of violence towards people, empathy towards animals does, thankfully, generalize to empathy towards other humans. Pets can help children learn both compassion and empathy.

Animals do more than teach children empathy. That in itself isn't so remarkable as children are known to have a natural interest and concern for animals. They have a touch of Eden in them and appear closer to God's original design when compared with adults. Edward O. Wilson, in his book *Biophilia,* suggests that humans evolved to have an active interest in the natural world. This should come as no surprise; a God who made us caretaker over the planet will instill in us an innate desire to be drawn into such a world. Many studies have shown that almost all children, if they do not already have a pet, [21] will ask for one at some point in their youth.

Animals influence the social, cognitive, and emotional growth of children. In 2011, researchers at Tuft's University found that dogs can help children with their reading skills. In this study children were divided into two groups; one who read aloud to a person for a half hour a week, and the second group who read out loud to a dog. By the end of the study, researchers found that the children who read to dogs increased their reading skills while the group who read to other humans actually experienced a decrease in their reading skills.

Studies on children show that they develop very strong emotional attachments to their pets. Pets are among the most important relationships in a child's life; allowing them comfort in times of stress and teaching them how to show affection. Children with low self-esteem are more likely to confide in a pet than a parent or friend, and more likely to gain confidence during adolescence. The pet provides them with a safe recipient of a child's innermost thoughts. A positive relationship with a pet can help children develop their non-verbal communication skills.

The inter-species relationship instills within the youth a sense of importance. A pet will continue to love a child even if that child does poorly in school or misbehaves. This teaches children unconditional love and affection. While at the same time, teaching children about respect for others; be they other animals or other humans.

****

Companion animals of a variety of species have been found to promote healthy emotional development in both neurotypical children and those with emotional, behavioral, or cognitive delays. Of course, it's not just children who benefit from the human/animal bond. Many adults have derived emotional support from animals as well. Animals as diverse as horses, pigs, and goats, to more typical animals such as cats, guinea pigs, and rabbits, and of course, most commonly dogs, have all helped patients cope with anxieties ranging from agoraphobia to PTSD and social anxiety and have helped people with depression and autism. Emotional support animals are not recognized as service animals under the Americans with Disabilities Act (ADA), therefore, they are not protected under laws protecting service animals. Nevertheless, patients do claim that they help provide them with cognitive, social, or emotional support.

Animals as psychological therapy is nothing new. 18th century Quaker philanthropist, William Tuck, ran an asylum for the mentally ill which he kept stocked with a wide array of different animals. [22] His goal was to help his patients develop good feelings, and a sense of responsibility and self-control with his menagerie. This idea spread throughout the 19th century, particularly in England. By the 19th century, Florence Nightingale was changing the face of nursing. She used pets with soldiers wounded by the Crimean War in what she dubbed "animal companion therapy." She found that small animals helped quite a bit in chronic patients.

Indeed, were it not for a dog she would have likely never become a nurse in the first place. Her first patient was a sheepdog who had been injured when cruel children pelted him with rocks. The impoverished shepherd who had the dog couldn't work without him and couldn't afford to keep a dog who didn't have a job. He was on his way to hang the dog when Nightingale persuaded him to let her try and heal him. She bandaged the poor dog's leg and within days he was himself again. Even thanking her by jumping on her and muddying her clothes. A "gift" we have all received from dogs from time to time. That same night, she had what she described as a vision from God instructing her to extend her gift of healing to others. She revolutionized the field of nursing and saved countless lives through her care and dedication.

The success of the experiments by William Tuck and Florence Nightingale, though not properly studied at the time, laid the groundwork for further exploration in the 20th and 21st centuries. Today many modern hospitals have active animal-assisted therapy (AAT) programs and much research is ongoing into efficacy of such programs. Current studies show that the use of animals contribute to the environments which better promote healing. The effects that animals have on the mind, body, and soul cannot be ignored. The growing body of literature on the healing and health effects of animals show that the bond is mutually beneficial.

****

In 2007, an article from the *New England Journal of Medicine* introduced people from all over the world to a tortoiseshell cat named "Oscar." As a kitten, Oscar was adopted by the Steere House Nursing and Rehabilitation Center in Rhode Island, a nursing home that specializes in dementia patients. While all cats are special, of course, Oscar is famous because he possesses a unique gift; one that no one else wants. He can accurately predict the deaths of the patients at Steere House.

Oscar is so adept, that he is actually more accurate than the nurses at predicting who will be the next to travel on their final journey. As a person dies, their cells release chemicals called ketones. A cat has between forty-five to eighty million smell receptors, far more than a human's five million. This superior sense of smell is likely what is alerting Oscar to the patients' imminent deaths. Oscar uses that information to the benefit of the patients at the center. He will curl up beside them and comfort them during their dying moments, purring and gently nuzzling them. Nurses at Steere House have learned to notify family members when Oscar lies near a patient, this gives the family time to come and say goodbye, or call a priest to conduct last rites. Oscar not only provides comfort to the patients during their last moment, but his presence provides comfort to their family as well. Because of Oscar, they can say good-bye, and they know that no one at Steere House has to die alone.

Oscar is not the only animal helping those going through a dark period. December 14, 2012, the nation was stunned when twenty year old Adam Lanza killed his mother, drove to Sandy Hook Elementary School in Newtown Connecticut, and killed twenty children, six employees, then himself. While a country mourned and struggled to make sense of the tragedy; charities and Good Samaritans rushed in to help. Among the helpers, is Spartacus Chooch, [23] often shortened to simply Spartacus. This 120 pound Akita and his person, Brad Cole, have spent hundreds of hours comforting the children who survived the massacre.

Spartacus is big, cuddly, and friendly. The children see him as non-confrontational; he will not judge them, nor will he question them, he simply listens. To the children who have survived so much in their young lives, he was just what they needed to work through their feelings as they learn to cope with the past trauma. A good hero never rests; when he is not helping the children of Newtown, Spartacus travels to hospitals providing comfort to the patients and their families there.

Spartacus is one of over seventy dogs serving the community of Newtown. The support and companionship he provides is invaluable. Spartacus, and others like him, have been so successful that Connecticut passed a new law that will provide trauma victims access to trained therapy dogs within 24 hours of a crisis. These volunteer response teams require dogs to have several handlers and be registered with an animal-assisted therapy organization. These animals will provide much comfort and support for people while they learn to cope with some of the darkest periods in their lives.

****

Dogs and cats have lived with people for thousands of years. The help and comfort that they provide to people wouldn't fit into this book. There are countless stories of them saving the lives of humans and other animals. Is it any wonder? The bond between cats and humans and dogs and humans is strong and unbreakable. So while it's great and wonderful that they help us and watch out for us, as we watch after them, it isn't really surprising. What is surprising, indeed amazing, is when undomesticated animals show altruism towards people.

Lions and humans have a rather checkered past. Both species have reasons to mistrust and fear the other. Lions have been known to kill and eat people, and people have hunted lions to near extinction. The two species seem to be natural enemies, but at least one pride of lions didn't get the memo. In Bita-Genet, Ethiopia, in 2005, a twelve year old girl was abducted by seven men. [24] She was repeatedly beaten by the men, who had intended to force her into marriage to one of them. The attack attracted the attention of a pride of three lions who chased off the men.

The lions stood guard over the child for over half a day before rescuers tracked her down. In contrast to the kidnappers, the lions didn't leave a scratch on her. When the rescue crew arrived, the lions merely went back into the forest; they knew their job was over. Skeptics claim that the lions were trying to eat the child, but wildlife expert with the rural development ministry, and leading British conservationist, Stuart Williams, believes that her cries are what saved her. Williams speculated that the whimpering could be reminiscent of the distress cries of a young cub, which may explain why the lions didn't kill her. The girl was treated for her injuries and returned to her family. Police were able to arrest four of the seven abductors, as of this writing, the other three remain at large.

****

Throughout history we have shown animals gentle care, careless disregard, and monstrous cruelty. When we fail at our job as caretaker; the Earth gets more polluted, entire species die out, and human lifespans decrease. When we take our role seriously; we clean up the air and water, wildlife recovers, we remove species from the endangered list, and human lifespans increase. The above stories are mere glimpses of the harmony we will have in paradise. We are currently very slowly returning to our original guardianship. Environmental regulations have cleaned up the planet to the cleanest that it's been in centuries. We are learning and understanding more about the natural world than we ever knew and it is beginning to recover. We understand more about other animals and how special they truly are, and as a result we are less eager to harm them.

We have a long way to go to come close to returning to God's original ideal, but we are making progress. We are now closer to Eden than any other period in history. Should we continue our course, and I think we will, all of the world will benefit. When we are at peace with animals we get back a little piece of Eden and we get a glimpse of the part of the world, and the community, that God declared "very good." We can rest in the security that even though things are getting better, one day we will return to paradise. In our future world, the wolf will live with the lamb, the leopard will lie down with the goat, the calf and the lion and the yearling together; and a little child will lead them. The cow will feed with the bear, their young will lie down together, and the lion will eat straw like the ox. The infant will play near the hole of the cobra, and the young child put his hand in the viper's nest. They will neither harm nor destroy on [God's] holy mountain.[1]

1   *Isaiah 11:6-9*

ON THE FIFTH DAY

EPILOGUE

From Genesis to Revelation, the Bible shows God's care and compassion for animals. They are not tools for us to use and abuse, God made them special in their own right. In Genesis God created animals and humans with the intention that we would live together in harmony and peace. He has promised us that in the new world we will recapture that unity. In the meantime, every time you stroke your cat's silky fur, or when you play fetch with your dog, or travel through forest glades on the back of a horse, or feel your heart smile when you watch an eagle in flight, you are getting a glimpse of the friendship and fellowship of God's original design.

When mankind fell from Grace we were punished. We had to work for our food, childbirth became painful, and we were banished from paradise. It didn't end there, unfortunately, for we drug the animals down with us. They didn't eat from that infamous tree of knowledge; therefore God provides all of their needs. Nevertheless, they were still punished. Those who believe that the creation myth and story of Adam and Eve is allegory, and those who believe it was historical, both understand the moral of this tale.

Instead of living in friendship with them, animals live in fear of man and fear of one another. Violence is an inherent fact of life that no species can escape. Aside from the obvious acts of violence which clearly hurts animals, I have to wonder if they suffer from the rift in our relationship as much as we do. There is a yearning in people to get back to nature and frolic in the fields with animals. We see it in Disney cartoons where the protagonist is invariably an animal lover. It is evidenced in the back-to-nature memoirs that top the bestseller lists and the movies where the hero connects with native tribes. There is a part of our nature that longs for the memory of Eden; do the animals share it too? Of course, we can never know the answer to that.

Throughout history, both individually and culturally, people have behaved like monsters or saints towards animals. The very best person you know has something in common with the very worst person you know: they're both people. We have the capacity for altruism, mercy, and love, even sacrificial love. Sadly, we also have the capacity for much evil, cruelty and barbarism.

All of humanity thrives when we embrace our role as caretaker to the Earth. When we remember that we are our brother's keeper, tasked with the welfare of all creation. On an individual level we are healthier, and on a global level, the whole of creation benefits when we act as guardians. Conversely, the whole world suffers when we reject that role. People become less healthy, both mentally and physically, there are greater acts of violence to one another and towards animals, and there's more pollution in the air and water.

God created land animals and humans on the sixth day. We were created together, and ultimately, we will all die together. In Ecclesiastes 3:19 King Solomon writes that the same fate awaits us both, and in verse 21 he questions whether the soul of man will rise upwards or soul of the animals will sink down. The very nature of the question takes for granted, howbeit, that animals have souls. The Holy Books of the Abrahamic faiths give instructions on how we are to be good stewards of nature. Many sincere people of faith have taken seriously the idea that animals are valuable to God in their own right. And many saints from James the Just to St. Frances Assisi have lived out their faith by their concern for animals.

By observing the other religions, we can see that they followed Noachide and some Mosaic laws concerning animal welfare. The founders of those religions may not have known of Noah or Moses, yet God placed a spark in their hearts and minds. Something as important as loving kindness and compassion for all life should not be known only to the followers of the Abrahamic faiths. Noachide laws were meant to be followed by all humanity, and God made sure that it was. Kindness and compassion rest within all human beings as a remnant of Eden. We long for it and take comfort in knowing that one day we will return to it.

We cannot escape the tug on our hearts when we connect with the outside world. Though 19th century ideals and technology tried to conquer nature in the name of progress, and current corporations try to destroy it in the name of greed, nature and wildlife has always had her defenders. Though we may have fallen from grace, there is still some humanity left in us, and it is often sparked by the love of our animal companions and the call of the natural world. We can take heart that we will one day reunite with the community that we lost.

ON THE FIFTH DAY

Glossary

Antediluvian The time period before the Biblical flood.

Anthropocentric The belief that human beings are the most important component in existence.

Biophilia The drive to connect with other lifeforms. The term was popularized in Edward O. Wilson's book of the same name.

Cartesian Of or relating to the French philosopher René Descartes

Corvids Latin: corvidae. The family of birds including crows, ravens, rooks, jays, jackdaws, magpies, nutcrackers, treepies, and choughs. They are among the most intelligent birds.

Exegesis A critical interpretation of text, usually scriptural.

Ex Nihilo A Latin phrase meaning "from nothing."

Interhuman Existing between two or more human beings.

Jainism An ancient, Indian religion that is rooted in Hinduism and based on the teachings of Mahavira, also known as Vardhamāna. Jains believe that spiritual purity is attained by practicing complete pacifism to all living things. Worldwide, there are approximately four million Jains.

Megafauna The large mammals, typically weighing over 100 lbs, of a geographical period, region, or habitat.

Misanthropy A wholesale contempt of the human species.

Myth A time-honored story, particularly one concerning the early history of a society, or explaining some natural or cultural phenomenon.

Lagomorph A mammal such as pikas, hares, and rabbits. Commonly misclassified as a rodent, their most common distinguishing characteristic is their double incisor teeth.

Laity Lay people uninvolved in the clergy or other professionals.

Neurochemical An organic molecule that aids in neural activity.

Neurotransmitter A chemical that is discharged at the end of a nerve fiber by the arrival of a nerve impulse that allows for the transport of another impulse to another nerve fiber, muscle fiber, or other structure.

Neurotypical An individual who displays a neurologically typical pattern of thought or behavior.

Nontrinitarian One who rejects the doctrine of the Trinity.

Prosocial Behavior that is positive, accommodating, cooperative, and intended to foster social acceptance and affiliative relationships.

Social Gaze A friendly gaze whereby the individual moves their eyes around an imaginary triangle of someone's eyes and mouth. This behavior has been observed in various social pack animals.

Sutra Sanskrit word meaning "thread" and used to refer to the sermons of Buddha and the aphorisms of Hindu Vedic teachings.

Theodicean adj. theodicy. The branch of philosophy that seeks to explain suffering in light of God's goodness.

Theory of mind The capability of assigning mental states; beliefs, objectives, desire, etc., to oneself and others. The awareness that another's state of mind may differ from one's own.

Trinity The Christian concept of one God in three persons: the Father, the Son, and the Holy Spirit.

Utilitarian The belief that actions are only useful if they benefit the majority.

Vivisection The practice of scientific experimentation on live animals.

ON THE FIFTH DAY

Bibliography

Introduction

(1) Kathleen McAuliffe, If Modern Humans Are So Smart, Why Are Our Brains Shrinking? Discover 20 January, 2011

(2) Fish count estimates, fishcount.org.uk, 2014

(3) About Cosmetics Animal Testing, Humane Society International, 2017

(4) CD Cameron, BK Payne, Escaping affect: how motivated emotion regulation create insensitivity to mass suffering, January 2011

(5) Gloria Grow, Pablo, *www.faunafoundation.org*

(6) Joseph D'Agnese, Elfie Semotan Discover Magazine, 1 December 2002

Chapter 1

(1) Karen Hardy, Jennie Brand-Miller, Katherine D. Brown, Thomas and Les Copeland, The Quarterly Review of Biology vol. 90 no. 3 September 2015

(2) Beth Timmins, Who Were The World's Very First Vegans? The Independent, 6, April, 2017

(3) Robert Dunn, Human Ancestors Were Nearly All Vegetarians, Scientific American 23 July 2012

(4) *Sample Registration System Baseline Survey 2014 censusindia.giv.in/vital_statistics*

(5) *Jo Ann Davidson World Religions and the Vegetarian Diet, Journal of the Adventist Theological Society (fall 2003)*

(6) *<u>Meat Eating Or Vegetarianism in Buddhism www.hinduwebsite.com/Buddhism/vegetarianism</u>*

(7) *National Jewish Population Survey (2001)*

(8) *Jasraj Suthar, Sufism and Vegetarianism 28 May 2015*

(9) *Steven Rosen, Food for the Spirit: Vegetarianism and the World Religions (San Diego: Bala Entourage, 1990) 108*

(10) *Cinzia Figus 375 million vegetarians worldwide. All the reasons for a green lifestyle. 27 October 2014*

(11) *Reuters, Americans pick pets over partner for desert sland poll,*

(12) *Pamela Cytrynbaum, Why Do Some Women Get More Comfort From Pets Than From Men? Psychology Today, 1 May, 2013*

(13) *Reuters, Americans pick pets over partner for desert island poll, 4 September, 2008*

Chapter 2

(1) *World Health Organization Global Health Observatory 2017*

(2) Bodie Hodge, Why Did People Start to Have Shorter Lives After the Flood. Answers in Genesis 16 July 2010

(3) W. Amos, J.I. Hoffmam, Evidence that two main bottleneck events shaped modern human genetic diversity. 7 October 2009

(4) Neelam Pandey, Hindustan Times, Manu's Flood was real, Saraswati nurtured Harappan settlements: Indian experts, 27 March 2017

(5) John Morris, Ph.D. 2001 Why Does Nearly Every Culture Have A Tradition of a Global Flood? Acts &Facts

(6) Qinglong Wu, Zhijun Zhao, Li Liu, DarryL E. Granger, Outburst flood at 1920 BCE supports historicity of China's Great Flood and the Xia dynasty. Science 5 August 2016

(7) Jenna Millman, Bryan Taylor, Lauren Effron, New Evidence Suggests Biblical Great Flood Happened, ABC News, 10 December, 2012

(8) Lydia Saad, Gallup, politics 4 June 2011

Chapter 3

(1) Top 10 Deadliest Animals, Lice Science, 30 March, 2016

(2) Joshua J. Mark, Ninevah, Ancient History Encyclopedia, 6 March, 2011

(3) Erika Belibtreu, Grisly Assyrian Record of Torture and Death, Biblical Archaeology Society, 2007

(4) Kathleen Mary Kenyon, Jericho, Brittanica 2017

(5) History in the headlines. War Animals from Horses to Glowworms: 7 Incredible facts 22 December 2011

(6) C. Douglas Stemer Home of Heroes 2014

(7) Alison Feeney-Hart, The Little-told Story of the Massive WWII Pet Cull, BBC News Magazine, 12 October 2013

Chapter 4

(1) Oxford- Lafayette Humane Society, United States Facts & Figures, animal over population, www.oxfordpets.com Viewed 20 July, 2017

(2) Moses Maimonides, Guide for the Perplexed, translated from the original Arabic text. Edition copyright 2010

(3) New World Encyclopedia Contributors, Judah haNasi, 6 September, 2008 www.newworldencyclopedia.org

Chapter 5

(1) Charles Q. Choi, Human Evolution: The Origin of Tool Use, Live Science 11 November 2009

(2) Virginia Morell, Animal Wise, How We Know Animals Think And Feel, page 44 Crown Publishing Group 2013

(3) Bill Wallauer, Exploring Evolution and Spirituality in Chimpanzees and Humans, Jane Goodall's Good news for all, 6 June, 2017

(4) Lin Edwards, Chimps dance in the face of fire, phys.org, 19 January 2010

(5) Rhawn Joseph, Ph.D, The Limbic System and the Soul, Zygon, the Journal of Religion and Science, Mach 2001

Chapter 6

(1) Charles Q. Choi, Prehistoric Cemetery Reveals Man and Fox Were Pals 3 February 2011

(2) Barbara J. Andrews, How Dogs Changed Human Evolution, 10 May 2016

(3) Tia Ghose, Dogs and Humans Evolved Together, Study Suggests, Live Science, 14 May, 2013

(4) Sarah Pruitt, Man's Best (and Oldest) Friend, History in the Headlines, 22 May 2013

(5) Joshua J. Mark, Dogs in the Ancient World, 21 June, 2014

(6) Stephanie Pappas, China Cat? Ancient Chinese May Have Domesticated Felines 16 December 2013

(7) Joshua J. Mark, Cats in the Ancient World, Ancient History Encyclopedia, 17 November, 2012

(8) David Zax A Brief History of HouseCats, Smithsonian.com, June 30, 2007

(9) David Grimm Ancient Egyptians may have given cats the personality to conquer the world. 19 June, 2017

(10) Rachel Nuwer, Domestic Cats Enjoyed Village Life In China 5,300 Years Ago, 16 December 2013

(11) Berkeley university "no more mystery meat" April, 2013 www.evolution.berkley.edu

(12) Swedish resource council "Domesticated Pig's Wild Origin Mapped" Science Daily 6 April 2005

Chapter 7

1   Judith Barad, Between the Species, 1988

2. F. G. Patterson, The Gestures of a Gorilla: Language Acquisition in Another Pongid. 1978

3. Savage Rambaugh, et al, Spontaneous symbol acquisition and communicative use by Pygmy chimpanzees, 1986

Chapter 8

(1) National Atmospheric Deposition Program

(2) London's Killer Smog, Royal Geographical Society, 2017

Chapter 9

(1) Adam Vaughn, Humans Creating Sixth Great Extinction of Animal Species, say Scientists, 19 June 2015

(2) National Park Service, U.S. Department of the Interior, USA.gov

(3) Douglas Croft, California Condor, Defenders of Wildlife, 2018

(4)   John R. Platt, *The Hawaiian Crow in Ready to Make Its Big Comeback*, Audubon Society, 5 October, 2016

(5)   *Annual Southern Sea Otter Survey: Despite Small Dip, Species Moves a Step Closer to Recovery*, U.S. Geological Survey, 29 September, 2017

(6)   *West Indian Manatee*, U.S. Fish and Wildlife Services, 1 May, 2017

(7)   Russell McCulley, *Louisiana to be the last state to ban cockfighting*, Reuters, 28 June, 2007

(8)   *A Closer Look at Dog Fighting*, American Society for the Prevention of Cruelty to Animals, 2018

(9)   United States Department Of Agricultural Office Of Inspector General 28 August 2008 Brian L. Haaser, Special agent in charge for investigations.

(10)   Animal Defense Legal Fund, *Animal Fighting Case Study: Michael Vick*

(11)   American Society for the Prevention of Cruelty to Animals, *Victory for Animal Fighting Victims: the U.S. Sentencing Commission Gets Tough*, 15 April, 2016

(12)   Joan Vannorsdall Schroeder, *The Day They Hanged an Elephant in East Tennessee*, 1 May, 1997

(13)   Kat Eschner, *Topsy the Elephant Was a Victim of Her Captors, Not Thomas Edison*, 4 January, 2017

(14) Agency France-Presse, Japan Kills more than 300 whales in annual Arctic hunt, 31 March 2017

(15) International whaling commission, whale population estimates, 2017

(16) Jim Peaco, Basic Facts About Bison, Defenders of Wildlife, 2018

(17) Diego Juffe-Bignoli, Ian Harrison, Stuart HM Butchart, Achieving Aichi Biodiversity Target 11 to improve the performance of protected areas and conserve freshwater biodiversity, 2016

(18) Larry Shannon-Missal, More than Ever, Pets are Members of the Family, 16 July, 2015

(19) American Pet Products Association 2017

Chapter 10

(1) D. Cracknell, M.P. White, S.Pahl, W.J.Nichols, M.H. Deplete, Marine Biota and Psychological Wellbeing: A preliminary Examination of Dose Response Effects in an Aquarium Setting. Environment and Behaviour 2015

(2) E. Paul Cherniak, Ariella R. Cherniak, The Benefit of Pets and Animal-Assisted Therapy to the Health of Older Individuals 2014

(3) E. Friedman, A.H. Katcher, J. J. Lynch, S.A. Thomas,Animal Companions and One-Year Survival of Patients, After Duscharge from a Coronary Care Unit, July 1980

(4) Ian Sample, Dogs can be trained to sniff out bowel cancer, Japanese researchers say, 31 January 2011

(5) Nicola J. Rooney, Steve Morant, Claire Guest, Investigation into the Value of Trained Glycemia Alert Dogs to Clients With a Type 1 Diabetes 7 August, 2013

(6) Suzanne C. Miller, Cathy C. Kennedy, Dale C. DeVoe, Matthew Hickey, Tracy Nelson, Lori Kogan, An Examination of Changes in Men and Women Before and After Interaction with a Bonded Dog, 28 April 2015

(7) Vilmos Csanyi, If Dogs Could Talk, North Point Press, 2000

(8) Annamarya Scaccia, Serotonin: What You Need To Know, 18 May 2017

(9) Interacting and petting animals created s hormonal response in humans that can fight depression, 2017

(10) Minho Nagasawa, Shouhei Mitsui, Shori En, Oxytocin-gaze positive loop and the convolution of human- dog bonds, 17 April, 2015

(11) Paul Zak, Dogs (and cats) can love, 22April, 2017

(12) Olga Solomon, What a Dog Can Do: Children with Autism and Therapy Dogs in Social Interaction, 11March 2010

(13) Gordon Hodson, Psychology Today, 19 June, 2012

(14) McGrath, Timothy Stephen 2013 Behaving Like Animals: Human Cruelty, Animal

Suffering, and American Culture, 1900-present. Doctoral dissertation, Harvard University

(15) Holly Nash, *Animal cruelty/human violence: the link, 27 June, 2001*

(16) *Animal abuse and human abuse partners in crime* <u>www.helpinganimals.com</u>

(17) *Karla S. Miller, John F. Knutson, Reports of severe physical punishment and exposure to animal cruelty by inmates convicted of felonies and by university students, 1 January 1997*

(18) *Susan McDonald, Childhood Animal Abuse and Violent Criminal Behavior: A Brief Literature, October 2011*

(19) *Rebecca Coffey, Lessons from America's First School Massacre, 21, December, 2012*

(20) *Peter Langman, School Shooters: The Warning Signs, Luke Woodham's Writings, school shooters. Info*

(21) *Gail F. Melson, Oxford Bibliographies in Childhood Studies: Children and Animals, Purdue University, 22 April, 2013*

(22) *Deborah Wells, The Value of Pets for Human Health, The Psychologist. 2017*

(23) *An Akita Named Spartacus*

(24) *Kidnapped girl 'rescued' by lions. BBC News, 22, June 2005*

www.ingramcontent.com/pod-product-compliance
Lightning Source LLC
Chambersburg PA
CBHW030646230426
43665CB00011B/978